Consider the *Lilies*

To Janet,
I hope you enjoy
this as much I had
writing it. You are
my inspiration,
Love, Terry

Consider the Lilies

A Faith-Filled Collection of Stories and Poems

TERRY HICKEY ABERCROMBIE

Inspiring Voices®
A Service of Guideposts

Inspiring Voices books may be ordered through booksellers or by contacting:

Inspiring Voices
1663 Liberty Drive
Bloomington, IN 47403
www.inspiringvoices.com
1-(866) 697-5313

Because of the dynamic nature of the Internet, any web addresses or links contained in this book may have changed since publication and may no longer be valid. The views expressed in this work are solely those of the author and do not necessarily reflect the views of the publisher, and the publisher hereby disclaims any responsibility for them.

Certain stock imagery © Thinkstock.
Any people depicted in stock imagery provided by Thinkstock are models, and such images are being used for illustrative purposes only.

ISBN: 978-1-4624-0033-1 (sc)
ISBN: 978-1-4624-0034-8 (e)

Library of Congress Control Number: 2011943039

Printed in the United States of America

WestBow Press rev. date: 11/17/2011

Contents

List of Illustrations

1. Pastel painting—Terry and Anne Hickey 1943
2. Oil on canvas—Michelle Lynn Mahrt
3. Oil on canvas—Shirlee and David Hickey 1934
4. Wayne Downing and Friends—newspaper photo
5. Wayne Downing—1944 photo
6. Angel sculpture
7. Pastel painting—Marjie Hickey Hull and rainbow
8. Chuck Perry—1971 photo
9. Oil on canvas—Cheyenne and Ethan Perry 2002
10. Lilies

Introduction

I have always loved to write—from the time I was a young girl—and was influenced by my Aunt Inez Killey, who worked for Women of the Moose of Aurora, Illinois as a writer and later, National Geographic in Washington, D. C. She died in 1946 of tuberculosis when I was six years old. My Dad, D. H. "Ham" Hickey was also a writer for harness racing magazines and eventually started his own monthly periodical, *The Standardbred Horse.*

My first poems were for greeting cards I made Mom for Mother's Day. At school, the teachers had some greetings already printed up for us to choose for the inside of our cards. One Mother's Day card I made had a sympathy message inside. Of course Mom never told me that I chose the wrong message. After the holidays Mom would give them back to me to put in my scrapbook.

It was only natural that I would continue writing as an adult. The oldest poem in my book was written when I was nineteen to my first husband and I continued to write even while raising my three sons. Whenever I had special people in my life, some devastation or happy moment, I would write poems or stories about them.

My large family and vast friendships I've had through my volunteering have given me much opportunity and inspiration to write about.

Most of the poems I've written were based on the theme of a particular greeting card that I used for the inside—for a family member or friend. It's a way of expressing how special they are to me.

I had also written some of my stories and poems for the opening of my talks for the singles groups, different prison ministries or a Cursillo team that I was involved with. When I volunteer, it seems like I get more blessings than what I give.

Dedication

My life experience with my family and friends was the inspiration for most of my stories and poems. Some have already gone to be with the Lord, some I haven't had the opportunity to spend a lot of time with lately, and some I'm able to see only on occasion that live close to me. No matter where they are, they have not been forgotten; for they have helped mold me into the person I am today and have brought me great joy. Without them in my life, there would not have been much to write about. My large family—one brother and six sisters—and friends have brought me so much happiness, as well as, most importantly, my three sons and six grandchildren that are truly the best things that have ever happened to me—besides my Lord—Who will always be number one in my life.

Epigraph

"Consider how the lilies grow. They do not labor or spin. Yet I tell you, not even Solomon in all his splendor was dressed like one of these. If that is how God clothes the grass of the field, which is here today, and tomorrow is thrown into the fire, how much more will he clothe you, O you of little faith! And do not set your heart on what you will eat or drink; do not worry about it. For the pagan world runs after all such things, and your Father knows that you need them. But seek his kingdom, and these things will be given to you as well. Do not be afraid, little flock, for your Father has been pleased to give you the kingdom. Sell your possessions and give to the poor. Provide purses for yourselves that will not wear out, a treasure in heaven that will not be exhausted, where no thief comes near and no moth destroys."—Luke 12: 27-33 NIV Bible

CHRISTMAS

Pastel painting – Terry and Anne Hickey 1943

The Doll in the Picture

My Dearest Daddy,

I don't quite know how to begin this letter. So much has happened that I don't fully understand. I try to put myself in your shoes, but it's impossible to do that. I thought that my only memory of you was that dreadful day when you and Mom had that big argument. When Mom died in 1986 (I was given two pictures—one of Anne and me on Christmas Day in 1943 and another of just the tree and our presents—and it jogged my memory a bit. I never thought that any picture would or could mean so much to me. I know that that is me in the picture, but I really don't feel like it is. It's like seeing it in a dream and that little girl sleeping isn't really me. Does that make any sense?

Anne named her doll Shirlee after our oldest sister. Shirlee named my doll after me—Fair Rosemond Terry. It was a fitting name for such a beautiful doll. We both treasured those dolls. I used to pin fabric around Fair Rosemond to make different outfits for her; then, when I was old enough to thread a needle, I started designing her clothes.

I noticed that the presents weren't wrapped. They were perfect presents, especially the doll. There are three dolls amid the other presents on the floor, one for us three youngest girls, Janet, Anne, and me. In the eyes of a three-year-old, that Christmas tree seemed magnificent, but looking at it now, it looks like there was only about one string of lights and just a few ornaments on the tree. How could there be, with a wife, one son, and seven daughters to feed?

I remember sitting for hours, looking through the tiny hole in the kaleidoscope at the pieces of color that seemed to dance into all kinds of exquisite designs. The clock on the console radio says 3:00 a.m. I guess that's when you took the first picture, probably right before you went to bed.

I recall the hours we'd sit around that console radio, listening to *Inner Sanctum* in the dark to make it scarier (per our brother Dave). Then there was the *Fibber McGee and Molly* show—did you know that they were from Peoria? The noise was horrendous when Fibber opened

3

his infamous junk closet. The clanging and banging was enough to set off a racecar at the Indy 500—let alone the hollering that Molly would do about how Fibber ought to clean it out someday *soon*. I can just about hear Molly hollering, "Fiiiibberrrrrrrr!"

Five-year old Anne is wide-awake—sitting on the floor beside me—engrossed in the Magic Slate and holding a doll like mine. I am in the large stuffed chair, sound asleep with my thumb in my mouth clutching onto a blanket. My other arm is wrapped around Fair Rosemond. I remember the black-and-white panda bear that's lying beside me also. There is a flat, rectangular-shaped box with pictures of boats and airplanes on it and titled Fleet—a typical present during World War II. There must have been a small war raging between you and Mom at that time that would soon invade the heart of a three-year-old girl, changing her life forever.

Daddy, I really have no way of knowing what part—if any—Mom played in your running around on her that subsequently led up to your leaving; but that's all in the past. I'm going to close my eyes right now and pretend that I am watching you picking out our presents for our very last Christmas together in 1943.

I see you, tall, thin good-looking, walking down the aisles of toys looking rather forlorn until your eyes catch sight of a beautiful doll. As you pick up the doll to look at it, you see that one hand is missing. You set it back on the shelf and start to walk away. Suddenly you go back and pick it up again. You start walking with it. I think you're searching for someone. Yes, you're looking for a salesclerk. You see a young woman straightening the coloring books. You walk over to her and show her the doll.

"I notice that this doll has a hand missing. I wonder if you would sell it to me at a reduced cost. I think my baby girl would love and treasure this doll even without the hand. I have eight children to buy for and only a modest amount of money."

"Let me see if I can find the department manager. I'll take the doll with me if you don't mind."

"Yes!" The clerk goes off to find her manager and explain the situation to him. The manager is very accommodating and says she can sell the doll for one dollar. She goes back to tell you that.

"Thanks!" You hand her the money plus enough for two more. She puts the dolls in a sack. "You've really made my day. Have a Merry Christmas!"

"You too."

Daddy, in my imaginary story, you were right. I really did love that doll. My enchanting memory was shattered to pieces that following spring. Anne and I were the only ones home at the time. You and Mom had gotten into a big argument. The dialogue that took place is unclear to me now, but the next thing I remember was Mom searching for her shoes so she could leave. Anne and I knew where they were, but you wouldn't let us tell Mom. That was very painful for me to see Mom hurt like that. Her shoes were under the chest of drawers in your bedroom. Mom finally left the house barefooted. She stayed with a friend, Lucille Grove. It must have happened sometime before Easter, because I recall the new coats and hats that Mom and Lucille made for us four younger girls to wear to church on Easter Sunday. Mine was my favorite color—blue.

Shortly after Easter, Mom came home, and you left. I had no idea the years that would pass before I would see you again. Eleven years had elapsed since the happenings in the picture took place until our next encounter at the funeral of Grossie How could a young girl of fourteen erase eleven years of heartache? I had no pictures of you so I couldn't even remember what you looked like. I doubt you would have known me if I hadn't sent you my school pictures. At night when I said my prayers, I always asked God if He would bring you back home so I would have a dad like all my friends had.

Daddy, I've heard so many bad things about you, I don't know what to think. I don't want to remember you the way everyone else does. I've been taught that there is some good in everyone. (Fourteen-year-old Anne Frank wrote in her diary while hiding from the Nazis in World War II, "In spite of everything, I really believe that people are basically good at heart.") But if that's so, why don't I have something good to remember you by? Sometimes I thought that maybe it would have been easier on me if you had died. Now, fifteen years after your mom died, your own death has come. It is so sad for me. As I looked at you one last time in your casket, I wondered who you really were. Were there other children in your life to take our place? Did you miss being a real father as much as I missed you being one? Will I ever know? I look for something of yours to grasp. Anything. I find nothing! At twenty-nine years old I still don't have a picture of you.

When All Will Be Okay

Daddy dear, I do recall that day so long ago
When you left our family with all your things in tow.
Daddy did you love me?
I really need to know.

Remember on that Christmas Day when I was only three?
When I woke up that early morn? That doll under the tree?
Did you know I missed you so?
Was that doll just for me?

I recall that panda bear all dressed in black and white;
Magic Slates so mystical so I could draw and write.
Dad did you remember that?
Was I your true delight?

Daddy, when you snapped that shot that morn a long time past,
Did you know that'd touch me so and make my memory last?
Dad did you remember it?
That time went by so fast.

Daddy, I have pardoned you for leaving us that way.
Did you really want to leave or did you want to stay?
Daddy is Mom with you there?
That's what I've hoped and prayed.

Daddy, when I get to heaven on that judgment day,
God will reunite us there, that's when to you I'll say,
Daddy I still love you too.
Then all will be okay.

With all my love, Terry

My Dear Terry,
I'll try to answer your questions as best I can. I have always loved
you. It was very difficult leaving all of you, but things weren't right

with your mom and me. I started going down to the local bar just for a few drinks. I met a woman there and I started going down there almost every night to see her. You may wonder how I could do that, but alcohol camouflages the way we think and look at things. Maybe I really didn't care if your mom found out. Maybe I thought that it wouldn't matter to her, but I was wrong. It did matter. I guess I didn't think about the consequences of my actions and that I might lose you kids in the process. After all, Catholics seldom got divorced back then. Nevertheless, that's exactly what happened.

I came to town frequently, but your mom wouldn't let me see any of you girls. Dave is the only one I was allowed to see. Of course he was the oldest so it wasn't such a problem to get together with him. I probably should have told you, but I guess I figured your mom had turned you against me anyway and maybe you might not have wanted to see me.

I used to talk about all of you to my friends. It was hard explaining to them why I didn't know much about you. It was easier to just tell them I had two kids—Shirley and Dave—rather than eight so they weren't so shocked that I left all of you. They always had a lot of questions. It was downright embarrassing. That may not have been the right thing to do, but it seemed right at the time.

I should have let you know when I got lung cancer. I really wanted to make things right with you. Maybe if you had known we might have had a few good years together.

One thing I want you to know is that I'm with the Lord now. He has a special picture book and videos that have given me the chance to view each stage of your life—including the two pictures of 1943. I assure you that I treasure every moment of your growing up. I saw your First Communion; watched you cheerleading for the St. Patrick basketball team when you won the championship. I saw your picture in the Peoria Journal Star that was taken at the basketball banquet. I saw your Confirmation; eighth grade graduation. I saw you in your automobile accident when you were sixteen. I saw your high school graduation and the pale blue dress with white daisies on it that you made for the occasion. I saw your wedding with your brother Dave walking you down the aisle; the wedding dress and veil that you made yourself; I even saw Chuckie, Curt and Todd when they were born.

The Lord has forgiven me for all of my mistakes. Believe me I suffered many years on earth from the consequences of those wrong doings. I hope you will forgive me and about that doll in the picture? I have Fair Rosemond Terry in my hands right now. She and I are here waiting for you. God has promised me that when all of you come to heaven—yes, I'm with your mom now—we'll all be a family again. I can hardly wait. Until then I'll be viewing all of your special events on earth from a very special vantage point.

Love, Dad

Daddy, as a little girl I thought Santa gave me that doll, but now I know that you gave me Fair Rosemond. I treasure that memory in the picture you took on that memorable Christmas so long ago in 1943. Sometimes I dream of being in heaven with you as a little girl. You're waiting with Fair Rosemond, arms opened wide, welcoming me and telling me you love me.

Treasures

Memories of that Christmas morning
Santa brought us gifts galore
Baby dolls sweet, cuddly panda bears too
Kaleidoscopes with colors that danced
Magic slates to draw and write on
All brought many hours of pleasure
But I must conclude that
Family and friends
Are my greatest treasure.

About D. H. "Ham" Hickey

My Dad, D. H. (Ham) Hickey Sr., was one of thirteen children and grew up on a farm in Bradford, Illinois where he first acquired his love of horses. Dad ran away from home when he was thirteen and lived with author John Hervey. Dad later edited his last book *The American Trotter* just before Hervey's death. He married my Mom, Marjorie E. Killey in 1926. When Dad left our family he moved to Indianapolis, Indiana where he worked as a photographer and writer for the *Horseman and Fair World* harness racing magazine. He also married Jerrie Barker while in Indianapolis, but they later divorced. He then moved to Santa Monica, California where he started his own magazine, *The Standardbred Horse Review*. He was highly regarded in the harness racing circles and was a critic for movies about horses. He critiqued *Home in Indiana* with Mickey Rooney and Jeanne Crain for *The Horseman*.

When Dad died in California on March 23, 1969 at the age of sixty-nine, my sister Shirlee told his best friend that she wouldn't be able to come back to Peoria for the funeral. His best friend was shocked that she wasn't coming home. He said my brother Dave would be the only family there. Shirlee said that all of her sisters would be there. That is when it came to light that Dad told people he only had two children, David and Shirlee. His friend was surprised Dad kept that information secret from him.

In the April 9, 1969 issue of *The Horseman* it was reported, "Word has just been obtained of the death of D. H. "Ham" Hickey, one of the sport's most knowledgeable students and writers about the breeding and accomplishments of standardbreds since the sport's beginning. The 69-year old harness writer died March 23 at Riverside General Hospital, Riverside, California, and burial was in St. John's Cemetery, Bradford, Illinois. Hickey, who had been in poor health in recent years, was at one time an editorial associate with The Horseman and later a steady contributor to the Harness Horse. In California, for several years, he published a monthly harness racing and breeding magazine, *The Standardbred Horse*. His thoughtful, interesting and accurate contributions to this and other magazines will be remembered well by our older readers."

The Turkey

Monday, December 6, 1982

I was having coffee with Russ Jones (who worked in the Allstate department at the retail store where I used to work). I told him about the turkey and champagne I won in the sales contest on November 22-23. I told him that I'd like to find a real needy family to give it to. I could use it myself, but I felt God wanted me to give it away—in secret. There are always people out there who are much worse off than me.

As I returned to my department, a young woman was waiting for me. She was slim with beautiful long black hair. She was looking for a decorator rug for her one-year-old boy to keep him warm while playing on the floor. I checked to see if any rugs were on sale, because the one she wanted was very expensive. It turned out that the particular rug that she wanted had a $100 markdown. That was great! She said that's what she planned to spend. Her husband had been laid off for over a year and was an alcoholic. I said, "All things are possible through God." Very shyly, she said, "You must be a Christian." I said, "Yes, I am and God sure can make a difference in our lives if we let him." She said she had divorce papers drawn up and her husband finally became a Christian. She hadn't been going to church much until then. We talked about a marriage not being complete unless God was at the center of it as in Ecclesiastes 4:12 TLB "Though one may be overpowered, two can defend themselves. A cord of three strands is not quickly broken."

When I wrote up the sale I found out her name and address. Donna Robertson shook my hand and told me how nice it was to meet me. *I could give her the turkey.*

Tuesday, December 7, 1982

Donna came back in with her husband and son and said her aunt had given them an area rug and she needed the money for groceries. She wanted to know if she could get a refund for the rug. I said, "Yes,

I'll give you a refund. She felt bad because she still wanted the rug. *I know for sure that she will be the recipient of my turkey.*

Wednesday, December 22, 1982

I enlisted my two young sons Curt and Todd to deliver the turkey to Donna. I found a small gift for each of them and a Christmas card to go along with the Turkey. I went by her house and pointed it out to the boys, then parked a block away and had the boys deliver it for me. I just signed the card, *From a Christian friend.* I felt so good that I was able to help Donna and her family. She would never guess it was from me. She'd never seen my boys before. It was very rewarding doing it in secret.

Thursday, December 23, 1982

I had the next four days off. I went to pick up my check at work that same day. I worked with a small regular salary plus commission. My checks varied from week to week. My check wasn't very good. I was very disappointed. When I went to my credit union to cash my check, I realized I was $75.00 overdrawn—How depressing! That only left me $35.00 for gas and groceries. I wanted to get a game or something for Curt and Todd. I had made velour sweaters for all three boys and bought them new pants and socks. I didn't know what to do. Tears kept rolling down my cheeks on and off all day. I tried to keep it from the boys. I didn't want them to know how bad things were.

Friday, December 24, 1982—Christmas Eve

Chuck called and wondered what I wanted for Christmas. I said all I wanted was for him to buy Curt and Todd something. He ended up buying them each a new radio/cassette player and T-shirts with decals on them. He used his whole paycheck. What a blessing that Chuck did that for them.

Saturday, December 25, 1982 Christmas

Chuck stayed at our house last night. We went to Mom's on Christmas day. It was a great Christmas day. We had a nice dinner and exchanged a few presents. I dropped Chuck off at his apartment at 6:30

p.m. When he started to leave he gave me a kiss and a hug. How elated I was. It was the first one since he was 12 or 13 years old. I couldn't quit thinking about it for days afterwards. Every time I thought about that, tears welled up in my eyes. I got the greatest gift Chuck could have given me. Nothing could have meant as much as that kiss and hug that Christmas night. I felt like that was my reward from God for giving something to someone else that I needed badly myself. I've discovered that when I'm really down—if I do something for someone else—it lifts me out of my despair. I praised the Lord that special Christmas! It all started with a turkey. Chuck's turnaround meant more to me than one hundred turkeys.

Oil on canvas - in memory of Michelle Lynn Mahrt
Dec 24, 1980–Oct 3, 1986

Christmas in Heaven

There is a place I long to be
Where earthlings have not trod
Where loved ones go when they leave earth
And see the face of God.

Where angels fiddle on their harps
And some on their guitars
Choirs singing joyfully
Drum sticks that shoot out stars.

When Christmas trees are decked in gold
With lights that shine so bright
They all will make my whole heart sing
Into the blissful night.

Someday there'll be a gathering
Of all those we hold dear.
When our lives are complete on earth
Then we can hold them near.

So when we get together to
Celebrate His birth
Think of the celebration
In heaven—not on earth.

VALENTINE'S DAY

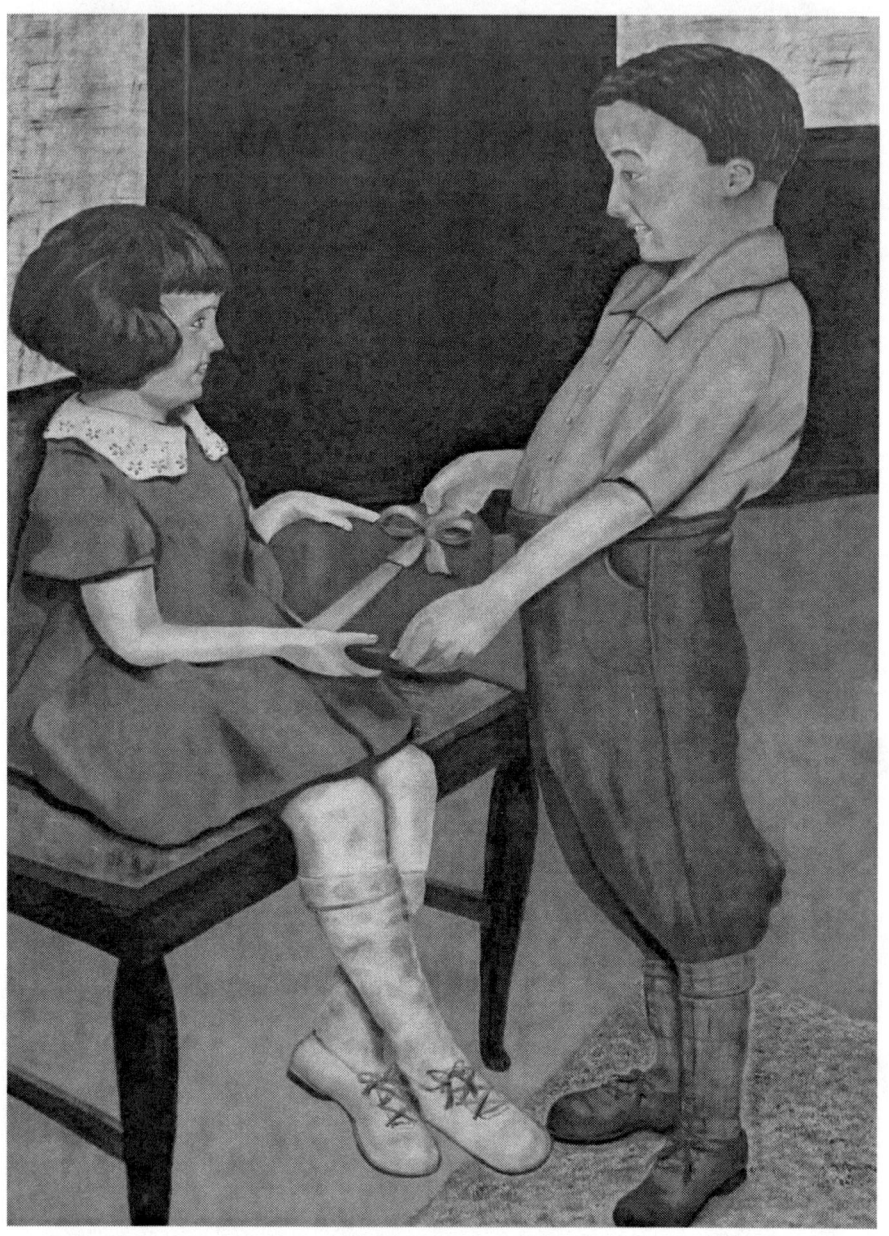

Oil on canvas – Shirlee and David Hickey 1934, both deceased

The photo was painted from the Peoria Star newspaper front page in 1934.
Used with permission of PJS.

"Will You Be My Valentine?

"All the sentiment of Valentine's Day is caught in the cover picture posed by David and Shirley Hickey, 2215 N Jefferson Street. Young Mr. Hickey acts perfectly the bashful swain despite the fact that the pictorial object of his affection is his own sister. He told the photographer that he was merely getting in practice."—*Peoria Star - February 14, 1934*

The newspaper photographer was a boarder at the home of Minnie Hamilton Hickey, the paternal grandmother of Shirley and David, who also lived with her. The photographer came to their door around 7:00 a.m. on Valentine's day and woke them up. He asked David if he would mind being photographed giving Shirley a box of candy. David said, "I'm not going to give my own sister any Valentine candy."

Despite the misgivings of David, the photographer was able to capture an adorable picture of them both.

Don't Be Fooled

Here's a box of candy, Sis
To brighten up your day.
You must give it back to me
When I, your brother, say.

'Cause this was not my doin.'
My friends would laugh at me.
I'd rather eat some worms
Or fall out of a tree
Than give my sister anything.
So don't be fooled by what I bring.

Valentine So Rare

I didn't have much opportunity to get to know my real Grandmothers. Mom didn't have a car and didn't know how to drive. Raising eight kids alone took up all of her money and time.

When I got married for the second time, my husband Larry's Grandmother Gladys was a wonderful Christian and I loved her right away. Later on when she was put in a nursing home, the boys and I visited her often—especially on every holiday. One Valentine's Day we had a very busy day ahead of us. We lived about 20 minutes away and would only have about ten minutes with her. My middle son Curt said, "Mom, why don't we visit her another day when we're not so busy." I wouldn't hear of that, because she was all alone and rarely had any visitors.

Gladys was in the community room when we arrived and Jimmy Binkele—a well-known Peoria entertainer—was playing the piano. While we were there for those ten minutes he played *In the Garden*; the song I planned to use for my Mom's pending funeral. Tears welled up in my eyes. What joy for me to hear Jimmy playing that tune while we were there. I knew why it was played at just the right time. I gave Gladys our card and a small heart-shaped box of chocolates.

Getting divorced from her grandson did not change Gladys's love for me one bit. She was a gift from God and one I will always cherish; for when I wasn't able to know my own, God gave me a lovely Valentine so rare—Grandmother Gladys—that I still hold dear to my heart.

My Valentine

I want to wish you husband dear
A happy Valentine's Day
And tell you of my love for you
That'll grow and ne'er fade away.

I love you as the stars above
Shine o'er the empty valley
As rain descends on hill and plain
And waters oats and barley.

I love you dear with all my heart
You are my beloved one.
We'll never part from each other
Till our work on earth is done.

My Everything

Dear Love, you fill my heart this day
With joy and happiness.
You give me courage, hope and love.
I long for your caress.

Kiss me in the still of night.
Embrace me tenderly.
Whisper sweet nothings in my ear
And dine and dance with me.

Keep me on your pedestal
High up o'er the plain.
Love me as you do right now
And there I will remain.

Your Child

Dear God, I saw You yesterday
I felt Your joy, Your peace, Your love.
I saw You in another man
And knew he came from up above.

He's gentle as a summer breeze
He has a warmth I've never known
His lips, his eyes, his caring ways
All tell me he's Your child alone.

My Endeavor

What an awesome world we live in.
Some people think hard to find,
But it is true. I know that now;
You have come into my mind.

You've brought me something special, dear
A gift I'll always treasure.
More precious than a pot of gold
Much more than I can measure.

Your gift is one of love's true bliss,
So great it's hard to define.
There is no way of seeing it,
But oh, how I know it's mine.

Dear Love, just spending time with you
Is such a special treasure.
I hope there's many more to come.
Your dreams are my endeavor.

The Reflection of Love

Can you define the meaning of love?
It's not very hard to do;
For love is all around us, just
As God made me and you.

I'll tell you of my thoughts on love.
It came through years of seeking.
I thought I knew it many times.
What joy when it came reaping.

It comes when you least expect it.
It peeks through those clouds of doubt.
And just when you think there is no hope,
It wanders in and takes its bout.

Love is Godliness most of all,
Not easily in detection.
I'm sure you'll find it just as I
By seeing through God, its reflection.

I knew He had a reason
For all the sadness I knew.
I found it just a short time ago.
I thank my blessings He gave me You.

ST. PATRICK'S DAY

An Irish Goodbye

Dear Friend, I know ye have no pain.
And peace? 'Tis yeers this day.
But I so longed to talk with ye,
Afore ye went away.

I'll miss that twinkle in yeer eyes;
Those devilish looks? Ah, yes!
But realize the warmth ye brought
Loved ones—Nevertheless.

Yeer wife put on a real great wake
I know she'd make ye proud.
McGinnis sang an Irish tune,
We sang the chorus a'loud.

So Friend please ready a place fer me
And keep the band in tune,
Just know that when I join ye there
I'll bring me own bassoon.

EASTER

Mary's Child

When Jesus came so long ago to bring hope to the world
He showed us how to live our lives. Such pain He did endure.
'Twas such a sacrifice for Him and really very sad
And how could Mary bear that sight?—the only Son she had.

But God in His great wisdom knew the future bright and true.
He gave us all His only Son to die for me and you.
I have three sons I love so much, if God would ask of me,
My dear I want one son to die for sins of the world. On a tree?

Could I do that, you just might ask. I surely could not do.
Take me instead, I'd want to say, but God would say, *Not you.*
God sent His only Son instead for all the world to see.
Chose Mary dear to bear His Child for faith and purity.

What hope is there for us today? It's Mary's hope in God
For all the hope brought by her Son in heaven we may trod.
Mary's hope is for us all. 'Twas Mary—the one who cried—
And cradled Jesus in her arms at birth and when He died.

FAITH

My Angel

Guardian Angel from above
Keep me safe…and the ones I love
Till we meet on the other shore
Where we will live forever more.

Now don't you tarry up in space.
I need you down on this earthly place
To guide me when I lose all sight.
Then tuck me safe in bed each night.

Special Effects

It was opening night for the Peoria Chiefs baseball team, a farm club of the Cubs, at Meinen Field. The sky was black and it had been raining for 1½ hours. I was with Barb Cundiff Johnson and Sister Pat (a Catholic nun). This was my very first time to go to a Chiefs game.

At the start of the game, we stood up to sing the National Anthem. As we started singing—with Dirk McGinnis leading and the Air National Guard holding our magnificent US flag—I noticed a small amount of orange appear beneath the clouds. As we continued singing, the black clouds started rolling up and away from the horizon exposing a gorgeous sunset. It looked like it was done on cue by a special effects person. Only the Master of Special Effects could have planned such a glorious spectacle.

Each Day with My Lord

I like to start each day with my Lord Jesus.
He lifts me up and helps me start anew.
He forgives the things I did wrong yesterday
And stands by me no matter what I do.

I love to share each day with my Lord Jesus
With all the friends He's brought into my life.
And I'm so glad I finally did surrender
My heart, my soul, my all to Jesus Christ.

My love for Him is perennial as the roses.
He guides me through each phase of life I cross.
No matter where I go or what I do
I know that when I stray, I won't stay lost.

I like to end each day with my Lord Jesus
And thank Him much for all He's done for me
For giving me the chance to share with others,
But most of all for letting me be me.

Big Dipper Blessings

What a beautiful June evening it was last night. I was at my favorite seafood restaurant—Jonah's—at the edge of the Illinois River in East Peoria. The food was superb and the outdoor temperature just right. Best of all I was with my special friend. I melted every time I looked into those expressive eyes—that danced gracefully like the sugar plum fairy in the Nutcracker Suite. They glistened like a prism as the falling sun shone on his face. Those eyes! I tried to imagine what they were saying, because he didn't share his feelings much with me. When I was in his presence, I felt so close to God. How I longed for him to tell me he loved me.

I think he was afraid to get hurt again. I prayed, *Lord, please tell him I won't hurt him. I truly love him. Some hurts are healthy and come with the territory. I was hoping the good things I have to offer him, would outweigh the bad. Sometimes it's necessary to step out in faith and take the risk. There are no sure things in life besides You, God. You are the essence of my very being, the Spirit of my soul. I'm still praying that You will somehow show him how much I love him.*

After my friend and I had dinner, we went walking outside along the riverbank and noticed a killdeer gracefully gliding as if it had no wings. The killdeer reminded me of him. I thought *Lord, please give him wings so he can fly.*

We went to an outdoor dance, Dancing Under the Stars at Glen Oak Park Amphitheater where a live band was playing. There were benches for people to sit on facing the concrete dance floor and the band. It was so romantic dancing under the stars with my friend. It reminded me of the outdoor dances at Proctor Recreation Center that I used to go to with my friends when we were in grade school. Back then the girls danced with each other.

I thought, *Lord, I truly felt Your presence as we danced under the starlit sky.* As we were leaving the dance, my friend looked up at the sky and said, "Look! The big dipper is watching us." I looked up and said, "Yes it sure is and it's brought big dipper blessings allowing us to soak up the awesome splendor of God and the universe."

I prayed, *Thank You, Lord for all the blessings I've received from You through him. Surround him in Your love and goodness. help him put the past behind and move on so he can truly experience Your blessings to the fullest. Your love shines through him like a lighthouse beckoning a ship to port.*

The blessings I received last night lingered on into the following day. I was on top of the world.

The Compassionate Encounter

When I walked through the door that day
I felt compassion in so many ways.
What I saw was such a surprise.
I saw Jesus in somebody's eyes.

Workers, mothers, children were there,
But one little boy had a cross to bear.
When I saw him I just had to impart
Compassion for him from the depths of my heart.

I'll never forget that encounter divine;
For it made me feel so very sublime.
And if you chance to see in a child
The face of Jesus so meek and so mild

Remember He's in all, the weak and the lame.
Just show compassion—that's why He came.
Yes, I saw Jesus in human fashion
Through that little boy and felt His compassion.

The keeper of an inn from long ago
Showed compassion for two strangers He did not know.
He knew nothing of Jesus who soon would be born
To Mary and Joseph that memorable morn.

His inn is known throughout the world o'er
To the well; the lame; the rich and the poor.
The compassion he showed for this Family
Will be in One History Book for all eternity.

THE SEASONS

Autumn Splendor

It was the middle of October. Autumn is a gorgeous time of year—perfect for taking a drive in the country. A friend took me for a ride to a log cabin that Abraham Lincoln once lived in in Springfield, Illinois.

As we were starting back toward evening, I noticed the sun going down in the west. As my eyes followed the beautiful sight across the sky, I saw that the reflection of the sun setting in the west brought out an array of color in the east; somehow reminding me of a disarrayed rainbow spreading its awesome beauty across the sky as it dissipated. How often in our own lives we are drawn to happy bright things and forget that it sometimes takes dull or troubled times to bring out the bright colors of our lives and complement one another. It's these contrasts that signify the most unique designs in weaving the fabric of our own lives.

I felt peace and contentment when I got home from my ride with my friend. I wished that I could have captured that scene before my memory faded as it would be replaced all too soon by some not-so-welcome signs of winter.

Winter Magic

When I look upon
The freshly fallen snow
Glistening like a prism
Spreading over the landscape,
I am in awe of its beauty,
Reminding me
To stop awhile
Soak it up
Build a snowman
Take time to chase the snowflakes;
For life can be like a snowflake
Made up of moments
That dissipate much too quickly.

Waiting for the Sunshine

Oh! It's so cold, dark and dreary.
When I go out I feel weary.
The sun won't shine just for a while.
Just to see it could make me smile.

Windows are iced up as can be.
Cars won't start even jauntily.
Everyone's sick with colds and flu.
Sub-zero weather makes me blue.

I can't wait till the sun comes out.
It will warm everything about.
Oh! To see the green grass and trees
And hear birds singing melodies.

It Must Be Spring

A butterfly flew in the sky
As spring opened its eyes
The crocus peaked out from the earth–
The start of paradise.

So many changes happening
It's everywhere I see
Springtime bursts in glorious hues
And birds sing full of glee.

I love the daisies in array
So pretty and so bright
All nestled 'long a garden walk
They're really quite a sight.

Spring is a gift I ponder much
When witnessing rebirth
I thank the Lord for giving me
This splendor here on earth.

When I have had the chance to view
A bluebird on the wing
Or rainbow stretched across the sky–
Ah yes! It must be spring!

The Wonderment of the Seasons

May winter bring you solitude
As God spreads His white blanket
Across the earth and trees
And freezes the rivers and streams
So as to capture their beauty
And store them temporarily
Only to bring them back again more vivid than before.

May spring bring with it
The many hues of the flowers
The rainbows
The birds to sing sweet melodies of love
The rapture of the springtime skies
The strong winds that bring the storms;
For it's through the storms we grow the most
And experience God's unrelenting gifts
Of contentment and love.

May summer bring you joy and solitude
For reflection of things already accomplished
Peace to handle each day
Love to pass on to others
And strength and faith
For whatever tomorrow might bring.

May autumn bring you God's beauty unsurpassed
With warm colors to surround you in His love
Allowing you to feel His presence
As He prepares you
For dreams you never thought possible
In the long winter days ahead.

MOTHER'S DAY

Hummingbird

What a beautiful sight to see
A hummingbird on the wing
Getting nectar from a flower
It tucks at my own heartstring.

How can a creature touch my heart
As this small bird has done?
Because it represents to me
Sereneness of the Son.

And for a Mother oh so dear
Whose love I treasure most;
Just like the hummingbird so rare
Of this I sure can boast.

But she—unlike the hummingbird—
Was always there for me
In every season of the year
To bring me lots of glee.

So when I see a hummingbird
I stop and soak it in
And thank my Mother oh so dear
Whose presence I take in.

In the Garden

In June of 1985 when Mom was hospitalized again with colon cancer my family asked me if I would plan her funeral. I was happy to do it.

On July 4th a friend of my sister Joanie's passed away after a two-year battle with cancer. I went to her funeral. It was one of the most inspirational funerals I had ever attended up until that time. The organist played one of my favorite hymns *In the Garden*. I hadn't heard it for quite a while. I'm so glad I was there to hear that song. As I drove back to my job I recalled how much Mom loved gardens. She could grow almost anything. Her house and patio were filled with flowers and plants. That was the perfect song to use for her funeral. I decided that I would ask two of my friends Rex Andrews and Mary Ann Fahey to sing that song at Mom's funeral. They both agreed that either one or both of them would do it if they were not committed to anything at the time.

In Kenneth W Osbeck's book, *101 Hymn Stories,* I read the story about the writing of the song *In the Garden*. Osbeck wrote, "It was in 1912 that music publisher, Dr. Adam Geibel asked C Austin Miles to write a hymn text that would be "sympathetic in tone, bringing tenderness in every line; one that would bring hope to the hopeless, rest for the weary, and downy pillows to dying beds" Miles was in his darkroom one day in March of 1912 and picked up his bible. It opened to John 20. "Mary Magdalene went to the disciples with the news: 'I have seen the Lord!' And she told them that he had said these things to her."—John 20:18 NIV. Miles had a vision as if he were transported back in time inside that very scene at the edge of a garden. The words came quickly to him for that beautiful, heartwarming song.

Sunday, September 8th I woke up for church and thought, *I don't want to go today.* I had trouble sleeping and I'd only had two hours of sleep the night before. Something inside me told me that I should go anyway. Little did I know what a special service awaited me. Two other friends J. Smith and Karen Page sang at the service. They sang *In the Garden*. The odd thing about it was that they didn't know anything about Mom having cancer or that I picked that song for her funeral. They did a fantastic job singing it as I sat in my pew crying during the whole song.

Friday September 13th I attended a weekend Mid-Illinois Christian Singles Enrichment Conference at the Peoria Civic Center. I had been doing some volunteer work for the conference the past month. Larry Heron from Oklahoma was one of the guest singers for the weekend. He has a wonderful voice. I was sitting in the front row right in front of him. The next thing that happened was almost too much for me to handle. Larry started talking real sentimental and I started crying before he even started singing "In the Garden."

I've never felt God working in my life so much as I did the past year. Before that time I was definitely too wrapped up in worldly things. Now I praise God for being in my life, showing me through other people and things how much He really loves me and will be with me in all the storms of my own life.

As Mother's Day drew near in 1986, I felt I had to write Mom something to make Mother's Day extra special that year as it would most likely be her last one. I wrote this special prayer and poem as a tribute to her:

Dear God, I have never told You this before, but there's something important I must tell You now. There is someone I have taken for granted most of my life. I thought she would always be here. She has sacrificed many things in her long life for me. She raised me with high ideals and a love of You. She never once interfered with my life. She only gives advice when I ask for it—and even then reluctantly. She sticks by me and believes in me. When I get sick she comforts me. When I get lonely she gives me hope. She's my best friend. She's like a flower that gets more beautiful with each passing day. She's My Precious Flower.

There is a special flower
That I am fondest of—
One that always blossoms.
One of eternal love.

I've had it for a long, long time.
I've watched it bloom and bloom.
In winter, summer, spring or fall
This flower is never doomed.

And do you know where it came from?
It came from up above.
Do you know why it never dies?
Because it's *Mother* love.

39

Yes God it's about time I'm finally getting around to thank You for my Mother. If You had allowed me to hand-pick her myself I couldn't have done as good a job. Her outer beauty is unsurpassed. Her inner beauty and love will be with me always. It's with sadness, but also great joy that I'll be able to give her back to You, because I know that the ultimate in living is dying and seeing You face to face in the ultimate Garden of Paradise.

A Mother to Remember

I once heard a speaker say
That the right mate will bring out the best in a person.
You certainly have brought out the best in my son.
I could have never found a better wife for him
Or mother for my grandchildren.

Your mother must have been an excellent example to you,
Instilling in you the qualities necessary to be a good mother.

My grandchildren are so lucky
To have such a special mother.

Thank you for bringing so much joy to my son!

GRADUATION/COLLEGE

God Bless You

You always know how to excel
In everything you do.
No matter what the task may be
You always pray it through.

The path you're taking is not short
Success we can't foretell.
But God will guide you all the way.
He knows you'll do it well.

You've blessed me with your caring ways
And special things you've done.
You willingly give of your time
And concern for everyone.

I have a special wish for you
Along with heartfelt prayers
That God will keep on blessing you.
No doubt I know He cares.

He'll lead the Way

A new chapter is coming your way
As you bid your books adieu.
Success will follow you soon enough
As sure as the sky is blue.

So know that I'll be praying for you
As you travel to new heights.
And if you stumble along the way
Just try to find new insights.

When life is not so complicated
Your future's so much brighter.
Numerous hopes and dreams can come true
The hard times will be lighter.

As you wander down this new inroad
I wish joy for what you do.
As you keep God foremost in your heart
Blessings soon will follow you.

College at Fifty-six?

I was at the campus of Illinois Central College (ICC)—a junior college in East Peoria, Illinois—to sign up for a non-credit Starting-Your-Own-Business class for desktop publishing. I had lost numerous jobs primarily due to fibromyalgia (a form of arthritis, but it affects all of the muscles and tendons in the body rather than the joints) which I developed in 1956 when I was sixteen after an auto accident. I injured my back and sprained both of my ankles.

Before the accident I made the honor roll several times. I paid attention in class and made good use of my study hall and often didn't even have to take books home to do homework. I got it done at school. After the accident my grades plummeted. The degree of pain I experienced was foreign to me then. I was unable to retain the information that I was being taught—no matter how many hours I spent studying. It seemed like the pain was overpowering my mind somewhat.

My senior year I was hospitalized and missed three months of schooling. Catholic schools didn't have tutors then and there was no time to make up my missed schoolwork. I was afraid I wouldn't be able to graduate and didn't know for sure until I received my diploma. My teachers didn't talk to me about it and I was too afraid to bring up the subject to them. I was so thrilled to see that I received a regular diploma on Graduation Day. I could have gone to Bradley University and it would have been paid for, but it seemed out of the question for me under the circumstances.

This day I was so overwhelmed. What was I doing there with all of the new high school graduates present? I needed to start a business so I would have a way to supplement my social security income. If I did something from my home, I could choose the time and how many hours I could handle working. My rheumatologist, Dr. Mark Getz said that, as a fibromyalgia patient, I needed to do something that allowed me to move around a lot.

The administration building where the registration was taking place was relatively easy to find. The main admission area was packed and there were very long lines at every counter with people registering.

When it was finally my turn to register I was sent to a counselor that dealt with older adults that wanted to go to college. I was told that I might qualify for a Pell or Map grant, but I needed to take at least six hours of credit courses. I chose an English class And an art class. I needed to take an English placement test so they would know what class to put me in. I was told to go to the building on the other side of the bridge. That sounded easy. I remembered driving underneath a bridge walkway not far from the administration building. The temperature was in the nineties that day and the humidity in Illinois can be difficult to contend with. I also don't do well in the sun anymore.

As I got closer to the bridge I could see that there was no place for pedestrians to walk under it. I thought maybe I was supposed to walk across that bridge not under it. I next walked across the bridge. The only building in that direction appeared to be pretty far away. I'm thirsty all of the time and usually take a bottle of water every place I go. I wasn't expecting to be out in the sun so long and I had no water with me. I was getting scorched in the sun. Tears were running down my cheeks and mixing with my sweat. I have a very light complexion and it probably turned scarlet red by that time. To add to my misery I developed a splitting headache.

I changed direction and started my walk to another building that seemed as far away as the first one. When I finally got to that building I realized that it wasn't the right one either. Now I had to turn around and get back to where I started, find an empty spot to sit on one of the benches lining the perimeter of the admissions area so I could rest, cool off and find someone to help me with the directions. There were people outside the administration building to answer questions, but no one knew what I was talking about. Some of the helpers—I later found out—were almost as new as I was.

I finally found the building I needed to be in for taking the English test. It was right outside and across from the administration building. The bridge the first person told me about was a bridge that connected the two buildings by where I started and was overhead. The area was so crowded with people when I arrived, that I hadn't noticed that I went under a bridge that connected the two buildings. I thought they meant a real bridge over a walk or roadway.

When I arrived at the testing room the women could tell I wasn't doing too well. They recommended I come back another day to take the test. English was always one of my favorite subjects so I thought *I've already been through so much.* I was determined to get it over with right then. I finished the test. The women told me I could take the English composition class. I wasn't sure what that meant. When I got home I told my son Todd about my ordeal. He said "Mom, you got to skip a class. That's a good thing!" That helped my disposition immensely. In spite of all of the stress that day I still did well enough on my English test that I was able to skip one class.

Going to ICC was one of the best things that ever happened to me in my life. Two of my three sons went to college and I helped them get grants and loans, but I had no idea that those grants and loans were available for me also. Once I took those first three classes I was totally addicted to learning. I went for seven years. I now have a total of 150 credit hours with a 3.51 grade point average. I qualified to join Phi Theta Kappa sorority, but, with limited funds that didn't seem like an important thing to do. I was just thrilled that I qualified. Currently I only need three more hours to get my graphic arts degree and fifteen hours for my graphic design degree.

My son, Todd moved from Colorado back to Peoria early in 2002 with his wife Teresa and their new baby Natasha; that following June I received my Desktop Publishing Certificate. I've been babysitting for him ever since. Juggling classes, caregiving—that I did before I started babysitting—and my volunteer work in four local prison ministries got to be too much along with all of my fibromyalgia pain. I finally decided to put my continuing education on hold along with the prison ministry. Todd has three daughters now and I thoroughly enjoy every minute I have babysitting with them as well as my limited time with my other three grandchildren that live in Fort Collins, Colorado.

Looking back on that ordeal I felt like a swordfish that conquered a giant whale through the help of my Lord and Savior, Jesus Christ. What seemed like an enormous undertaking was in reality just another, but important chapter in my life with God guiding me all the way. I am so grateful.

WEDDINGS/ANNIVERSARIES

I Do

A wedding is a sacred time
For family or friend
To join you in your happiness
Where your two lives will blend.

It's time to set aside old things
And start your life anew.
There will be things that won't seem clear
Until you walk them through.

But know you'll never be alone
With best friend at your side
And though each joy adds up times two
Each sad time will divide.

On this day when you say *I Do*
I wish you all the best
Of what life has to offer you
And may your lives be blest.

God grant you all you hope for
And more than that I pray
To a very special couple
On your glorious wedding day.

A Mother's Wedding Prayer

My son, you have now come to a new chapter in your life. I'm so proud of all you've accomplished. I've been praying for a long time that God would bless you with a special Christian woman to share your life with and I'm thankful that my prayers have become a reality. I know you waited quite a while, but God was preparing you all along for just this very moment when you will be united in Holy matrimony.

When I first saw you the moment you were born I thought *what a beautiful precious baby!* I could not anticipate the joy you would bring to my heart until that very moment. I felt honored and blessed to be given such a wonderful gift; for it truly is a gift to be one with another and then to experience the birth of a precious little baby created by God.

I tried hard to be a good mother, but a lot of things in life we don't seem prepared for until they actually happen. Parenting is a lifetime process that we learn each step along the way. The heartaches were well outnumbered by all the joys you've brought into my life and that's an awesome feeling.

My prayer for you today is that God will bless you and your new wife and allow you to experience that special miracle bestowed on me so many years ago—the birth of your own children. Only then will you truly experience just how I feel about you deep down in the depths of my heart.

Forever in Him

On this day as you celebrate
The day when you were wed
'Twas not so very long ago
When hence those vows were said.

I watched your love grow day by day.
I've seen it under stress.
But you have shown the strength of yours
You shine above the best.

How could I know how wonderful
You'd be as parents true?
Or that your love would grow so strong
And oh so caring too?

I think the reason for success
Lies in this simple fact;
That first and foremost being friends
Keeps everything intact.

What I wish for you soul mates most
—And also what I pray—
That each new day God will bless you
Forever along the way.

The Magical Wedding Box

When things don't seem to go so well
And there's no hope in sight,
The magic of the wedding box
Will bring a gleam of light.
Just find a box—any size'll do
And place your hurts inside.
You could add a little tear
Then softly wipe your eyes.

Gently place the lid on top and
Wrap with a ribbon blue.
Next attach two bells to that—
One bell for each of you.
Now close your eyes and say a prayer.
Then listen with your heart
Until you hear the sound that
The wedding bells impart.

Their music is so sweet a tune
That troubles disappear.
Because of the precious wedding box
You'll hold each other dear.
Without your troubles deep inside
The magic would not be.
And you might not find the reason
Jesus died for you and me.

When your children are all grown up
And they decide to marry,
Please tell them of the wedding box
For it's extraordinary!
Explain to them the utmost need
For Jesus Christ Our Lord
For they must find Him as you did.
Heaven will be their rich reward.

Loving Reflections

Sometimes we get so busy in our daily lives
That we forget about
How special our loved ones are
And of all of the happiness
They've brought into our lives.

But then when anniversaries come around
It's a good time
To reflect on the passing years
And how empty life seemed without them
And all of the fundamental qualities
They've added to our complicated lives.

Soon you'll have another special someone
—A daughter or son—
To share your lives with.
May the outpouring of love
That you share for one another
Flow out into all of your children
And their children
For many years to come.

FATHER'S DAY

A Real Father

A Father is one that helped support you
When you were growing up.
One who walked you down the aisle
On your wedding day.
One who taught you many things
That you didn't learn in school.
One who gave you lots of advice
That stayed with you to this day.
One who is so smart it's hard to believe
He only had 8½ years of education—
You'd swear he went to college.
One who idolizes your children
And your children's children.
This father had no birth children of his own
He is really my brother,
To me he's a *Real* Father
In every sense of the word.

A Really True Cub Fan Is...

One who is outnumbered ten to one.
One who stays true to them
No matter how many games they lose.
One who waits a lifetime
For them to win the World Series
And keeps saying *maybe this year...*
Have a great Father's Day—
And—*maybe this year...!*

Reminisces of a Brother

I cannot believe that it is Father's Day again.
It seems that they are passing with a frequency
Similar to the changing of the seasons.

What was it like when Mom would come home
After having another baby
When all you heard was *It'sgirl*—seven times?
When I was a little child, you appeared so tall
Strong and wise
I thought you knew everything about anything
And you probably did.

Now that I'm older I feel the gap between us
Diminishing as surely as the sun sets on the horizon
And I look back fondly on all the things you've accomplished
Especially for being a surrogate dad to me.
My wish for you today is that you enjoy
This Father's Day as no other.

Fishing Paradise

There's nothing like a quiet night
Watching the hot sun go down
Along a blue, calm mountain stream
Not far from the edge of town.

Just close your eyes and picture it
As your dream takes you away
Catching the biggest fish—Oh, yes!
—the largest one of the day.

And then it's time for you to eat.
So cook up that fish you caught,
Along with bread and butter.
Now contentment you have got.

Remember all the trips you took
To get to that far-off place?
Cherish the time that you once had
Paradise—so full of grace.

For a Son on Father's Day

On this day that commemorates
A father tried and true
You represent one of the best
So don't you dare be blue.

For our God in all His wisdom
Chose you for such a feat
To be the dad of three sweet kids
A dad who can't be beat.

For a Special Daddy

Mommy tells me that today is Father's Day.
I cannot let the day go by
Without wishing you a *Happy Father's Day*
To my favorite Daddy.

You are the best Daddy a little fella could ever have.
When God asked me who I wanted for a Daddy
I told Him I wanted you
He asked me why? And I said
That you would be as wonderful to me
As any daddy could be.
I was right and I couldn't have
Picked a better daddy
If I'd combed the world over.

When Mommy wants me to take a nap
You always want me to stay up
So you can play with me.
When Mommy says I can't have any candy
You put it in my mouth when she isn't looking
Mommy gets so angry
But I smile real big so she's not angry anymore.

Sometimes when you go to the store
You take me with you.
You throw me up in the air
Till my head touches the ceiling.
You put me in bed with you
So I can wake up Mommy.
She gets real angry.
But I just give her that little impish smile again
And make her smile too.

So Daddy on your special day
I want to wish a Happy Father's Day
To the best daddy in the whole world—
My Daddy—with love from Your Little Man.

MILITARY

Four-star General Wayne Allan Downing

The Young Wayne I Knew

I first met Wayne in the summer after eighth grade graduation—at the Catholic Youth Center (CYC) at Spalding. The girls went to the Academy of Our Lady across the street. Most of the sports and dance activities were combined, but school time was separate. (I think they thought we'd get more schoolwork done without distractions from the boys). The CYC was great, because we were able to meet the boys from Spalding and dance together, or just hang out. The center was open every Friday night and usually after sports events. The center also had a snack bar and some table games, but all I wanted to do was dance.

Wayne took me to the back-to-school dance when we were freshmen in the fall of 1954. I bought a new outfit with my babysitting money; a black wool jumper with a v-neckline and semi-flared skirt and I wore a light pink and deep rose-print fitted Lady Manhattan blouse to wear underneath.

Wayne's mom, Eileen Downing, didn't drive at the time, so she enlisted her sister (Wayne's Aunt) to drive him to my house to pick me up, then dropped us off at Kramer's restaurant for supper where we had their famous tenderloins. (That restaurant later became Jumer's Castle Lodge where my family had many wonderful get-togethers while my Mom was alive). His Aunt picked us up after our supper and took us to the dance, then had to pick us up when the dance was over and take me home. I had such a great time. Wayne was one of the nicest-looking and popular boys in the freshman class with a great personality. I felt honored that he invited me to the dance. Wayne was very reserved and didn't try to get attention. Of course, he didn't need to. His mom said he had a special charisma even back then and I agree with that.

THE PURPLE IRISH. Spalding's 58'ers, six seniors with purple-painted faces, led the all-male enrollment school's cheering section in roaring fashion throughout the 58 to 49 victory over Highland. The boys who started cheering for the "Fighting Irish" on a "volunteer" basis at the start of regional play painted their faces with water paint that "should last two days" or duration of the Elite Eight tourney. Group includes, seated, left to right, Tom Joyce, Tom Palmer, Wayne Downing; second row, Jay Vonachen, Bob Rehm and John Schlenker.

Wayne Downing and Friends 1958

Wayne & the Purple Irish Cheerleaders

Our Spalding basketball team went to the Illinois High School Association (IHSA) state tournament our senior year in March of 1958. We had a wonderful team—Seniors Dave McGann, Dave Skender, Mike Haley, Don Molitor, (from the junior class, Willie Payne)—and both of our schools were so proud of them. We ended up third highest in the state.

Wayne and some other guys used water paint to paint their faces and hands purple, donned white hats with purple garland for decoration, white shirts, purple pants and their white ties trimmed with purple with an 'S' for Spalding—that were part of their Spalding school uniforms—and did cheers for the four games we played against Ottawa, Highland, Rock Falls and Aurora West. It was so much fun watching them cheer. They told the newspaper that they were working on a *volunteer* basis.

Three seniors from the Academy of Our Lady were cheerleaders for Spalding—Judy Dunne, Rita Armitage and Mary Jo Lintz. They did a fabulous job. The picture of the Purple Irish Cheerleaders was featured in many of the newspapers throughout the state of Illinois. The guys just added to the excitement we all felt from placing so high in the state tournament our senior year. At the super sectional games that were played in various cities throughout the state, the Spalding/Ottawa game was played at Bradley Fieldhouse in Peoria. We had more people in attendance than any of the other teams. We had over 8,000 fans present. Peoria is a great basketball town.

When I see that picture of Wayne with purple paint on his face, I think of the contrast of the color he put on his face during very dangerous combat missions throughout his stellar career in the Army.

Wayne and the Pigeons

Just before the start of the Spalding-Ottawa game, Wayne and two other guys released some pigeons with purple and white streamers, our school colors, tied to their legs. Through the years it's always been a mystery to our class and the priests at Spalding about who the culprits were and how they accomplished the fete. This is their story that wasn't revealed until 2010, fifty-two years after the fact:

"Wayne Downing, Herman Weber, and his younger brother, Oscar Weber went to the old Shierer's or Stafford's Dairy barn (that sat back off the road) on University—by where Culver's is located now—late the night before the game. Wild pigeons nested there. They had flashlights with them and shined the lights in the pigeon's eyes to blind them so the guys could pick them up with no trouble. Each of the guys took two pigeons and put one in each of their jacket pockets and that's where they stayed until the game the next day. When birds are in complete darkness they don't make any noise.

"The next day right before the game the guys tied purple and white crepe paper streamers onto the legs of the pigeons. They put the pigeons back in their pockets to wait for the start of the Spalding/Ottawa game at the Bradley Fieldhouse. We won that game. Next it was on to Champaign for the Spalding-Highland game, the Spalding-Rock Falls game (we lost that one), then the Spalding-Aurora game that cinched the third place trophy. After the first game, the guys were afraid they'd get caught if they used just purple and white colored streamers again, so they added the colors of the opposing teams as well—that way no one could prove that it was Spalding guys that did it for sure. The principal of Spalding, Father Charles Williams, denied to the PJS newspaper that the pigeon fiasco was done by one of his Spalding students. He never found out otherwise.

The Funeral—Saturday, July 21, 2007

I arrived thirty minutes early at St. Thomas the Apostle Catholic Church in Peoria Heights for the funeral service. There were no more parking spaces in the parking lot when I arrived and I was directed to drive to the Peoria Stadium—where we used to have our football games in high school—and there would be a bus waiting to transport people back to the church. There were two buses from the 183rd infantry waiting to transport people. I got on one of the buses and sat there for about fifteen minutes. No one else showed up. I finally said that if we waited much longer I wouldn't be able to find a seat. One of the infantrymen agreed to take me on his bus. I had the whole bus to myself. Can you beat that? Just as I thought there were no seats available in the main part of the church. I was directed to a chapel at the back of the church where a large viewing screen was set up above a small altar.

The funeral service was celebrated by our Bishop, the Most Reverend Daniel Jenky along with Reverend Thomas Taylor.

After listening to all of the wonderful stories about Wayne by the Reverend Thomas Taylor, billionaire Ross Perot, West Point graduate and founder of America Online Jim Kimsey, Lt. Gen. Robert Wagner—the commander of the Army's elite Green Berets and Rangers—and Marlianne Downing Fortune, I learned another side of Wayne that I hadn't known. Some of Wayne's West Point classmates of 1962 were there. Hebrews 13:2 TLB says: "Don't forget to be kind to strangers, for some who have done this have entertained angels without realizing it." God certainly put a mighty angel in our midst. Now he can guard us from a different vantage point. *Take care secret warrior. Great job!*

The General Salutes
Wayne Downing, four years old December 15, 1944

Memories of Wayne
By Marlianne Downing Fortune (deceased)

"We have heard stories of Wayne as a friend, a cadet, a soldier, a father, and a colleague. My stories of Wayne are as a "big brother" and also my first friend. I think I was his first friend, too. There was no one else to be his "troops", and I was a willing participant. (You don't learn to be a commander by talking to yourself.)

"I even played "Strategy" with him. The goal of the board game was to take a town, which was surrounded by mountains, rivers, and lakes, and keep it. To keep me playing, Wayne would always say, "I think you might win this one."

"One year, Wayne received boxing gloves for Christmas, and that very day I was learning to spar. Mom kept saying, "Don't hit her. I don't want her getting hurt." Wayne answered, "I won't hit hard. See, she won't even feel it." And I didn't.

"After the boxing, Mom was more willing to let me play in the neighborhood football games. If they were short a man or two, I would fill in. So I learned to hit low and drive my head into my opponents' stomachs.

"My memories of growing up with Wayne can't be erased. To entertain at family events, Wayne, Becky, and I would make up our own radio programs, complete with commercials, to keep the family laughing.

"A talk about Wayne would not be complete without talking about our mother. Wayne always included her when he spoke, because he knew he would not have become the man he was without her. At 24, she was left to raise three children (ages 1½, 3, and 4) by herself. Many of Wayne's traits he got from Mom. Believe me, she ruled our house with an iron fist. If you had known Wayne in high school, you would know why this was necessary.

"Wayne took his role as "big brother" seriously. One day after school, as we were riding our bikes, a boy from my fourth-grade class intentionally rammed my bike with his and knocked me to the ground. I had a quick temper like Wayne, so I got up and pulled the other kid off his bike. I had him on the ground and was beating him with my fists when Wayne came along and pulled me off. Wayne gave me hell because, according to him, girls aren't supposed to hit boys because they can't fight back. My answer was that I couldn't wait for him to beat the kid up for me.

"Much later, after Wayne went to West Point, I found out that he had told the other boys in my high school that no one could ask me out unless they got his permission. When I found out afterwards who his "rejects" were, I realized he was looking out for me.

"Wayne also made it easy for me to fly "under the radar". By comparison, I always looked like an angel, although I vicariously enjoyed his exploits. Like going to Cuba with two friends when he was 16. That was when Castro was fighting in the hills, and Batista stilled ruled. How did he do it? As you probably know, when Wayne had a goal he reached it.

"During his senior year, the Spalding basketball team made it to the final 16 in the state tournament. These games were always played ad Bradley Field House with lots of media coverage. Very exciting. At some point in the second half of the game, there was a big commotion as hundreds of pigeons flew up to the rafters. They all had purple and white streamers (the school colors) tied to their legs. No one ever figured out how this could have happened since security was very tight, but the stunt Wayne and his cohorts written all over it. Nothing was ever proven, nor was anyone talking. It was fun being his sister. I was very proud of him.

"When I was in high school, I would never have thought of calling him a diplomat. One evening, he said to Mom about my sister, "You aren't going to let her go out looking like that?!" She looked fine – very pretty – but she spent the rest of the evening worrying. Another big brother role – making sure we were presentable.

"At his graduation from West Point, he fixed us up with guys from his company. I'm sure he worried before we got there, but I guess we passed. He actually told Mom that we looked great and that he had received a lot of compliments about his pretty sisters. Remember, that was over 40 years ago. And Becky was a really beautiful girl.

"Wayne was a great "big brother" and always had our best interests at heart."

Later in life Marli convinced Wayne to take her up in an airplane and let her jump out of an airplane. As Marli was getting ready to jump, Wayne said to Marli, "Mom's going to kill me if anything happens to you." They didn't dare tell their Mom about the jump ahead of time. Marli liked it so well that she jumped again that same day.

Eulogy—Funeral in Peoria, Illinois

Brian McEnany, USMA Class of 1962
(with assistance from Bob Meceda and Don Kauer),
posted on USMA website-used with permission

"General Wayne Downing—classmate, company mate, retired-4-star general, former Nat. Security Advisor for Terrorism, Commander of all Special Operations Forces and NBC news analyst, passed away this week. A memorial service was held in Peoria, Illinois—his home town—at St. Thomas the Apostle Catholic Church.

"Thirteen of us climbed into a Gulfstream at Dulles at 0745 this morning – Jim Kimsey, Denny Reimer, Jack Reavill, Phil Stewart, Harry Hagerty, Art Bondshu, Brian McEnany, John O'Neal, George Handy, JJ Heigl, Bob Meceda, George Kirschenbauer and Jack Nicholson from the Class of 56—and CEO of the American Battle Monument Commission also came. Brian Williams' moving tribute to Wayne was played on the plane ride to Peoria. It generated a lot of conversation and remembrances of Wayne for the rest of the trip.

"1 hr 45 min flight—smooth and level—dropped us into the green, flat, agricultural lands around Peoria—the heartland of America. The city, nestled on the banks of the Illinois River, had turned out to honor one of its own. Flags flew at half-staff, the local police controlled the routes in and out of the church area.

"St Thomas is a huge Catholic church and it was filled by 10 AM. Classmates sat in two rows reserved for us. High white ceilings—sunlight streaming through the large stained glass windows, lit up the interior of the packed church. Violins and trumpets played before the mass began—a fine tenor and choir sang during the service. And it was a wonderful service.

"The priest, the Bishop, clad in maroon and carrying his staff, the girls and boys carrying the Cross, Bishop's crook and candles proceeded to the front of the church. Then, multi-colored berets of the honor guard, all Senior NCOs carrying Wayne's casket marched behind. Sharp, crisp uniforms with bloused trousers, spit-shined jump boots—chests filled with rows of ribbons. There were nine pallbearers—Two Marines, Two Navy, Two Air Force, Two Army and was led by an Army NCO—all Special Ops. Sprays of flowers from the various Special Operations Commands laid across the room and the big, red SOCOM patch leaned against the altar. The memorial program was filled with Wayne's career assignments—"Rangers Lead The Way" emblazoned across the bottom of one page, the Ranger Creed printed on the back cover.

"Several more classmates showed up at the church—Don Kauer and his wife, Jim McQuillen and his wife, Phil Burns, Ralph Lurker—a few others whose faces I recognize, but forgive me, their names escaped me. I think about twenty of us sat down in two rows near the front. The audience was filled with brass—each of the service Special Ops chiefs—3 and 4-star generals—was present along with their retinues. All names you would recognize. The Army's Special Ops CSM Hall and its commander were present. I do not believe there was any representation from the White House, but I could be mistaken. A few other gray-haired gentlemen in suits, past members of the legion of shadowy warriors, crowded into a few more rows. Also in attendance was more than one former member of Wayne's various commands on crutches. Wayne's extended family filled the rows on the right. His mother, Eileen and his wife, Kathy, were escorted to the front.

"Brian Williams and the NBC news and camera crew sat right behind us. I had a chance to talk with Brian Williams after the service and thanked him for the wonderful tribute he gave Wayne on NBC News. He seems like a good man—firm handshake, listened to what we were saying. His father had been an Army Captain. Several of our group also thanked him for his words. Later, as we walked together into the parking lot, he told me that he and his wife will be at West Point for the funeral on Sept 27th. He was appreciative of our thanks for his tribute. One of the guys told me later that Williams told him that he looked at the two rows in front of him in the chapel and could see the Long Gray Line.

"The readings came from two of the family and then, three of the grand-children stepped up to the mike and read the prayers in their clear, children's voices—they bore the gifts to the altar a short time later.

"The priest spoke as if he knew Wayne during the Homily—He choked up at one point so I think they were friends. The Eulogies were given by H Ross Perot, Phil (Kathy's son), Jim Kimsey, and LTGEN Bob Wagner the head of the Army's Special Ops Command.

"Perot, still erect and proud, loudly spit out his words, punctuating them with quotes from various more famous people. He paraphrased Churchill's "Never Quit, Never, Never," quoted during WW II in relation to Wayne and his approach to operations. He talked about some of the projects where Wayne helped get immediate care for soldiers or helped get people out of harm's way—When questioned about what happened, Wayne always replied, "Perot, you don't want to know how I did it..."

"Phil presented a family side of Wayne that most of us never knew. He loved being back in Peoria—tales about clothing his daughter in North Vietnamese officers uniform and sending her off to trick or treat or inadvertently filling up the rental car in Europe with gas when he should have filled it with diesel during one trip.

"Jim's talk was heartfelt. He spent many hours and days with Wayne on various projects. He had just come back from Israel with him only two weeks ago. He spoke about his friendship and said, "Wayne led the world's most lethal fighting force, and was its most compassionate man..." He finished with words that most of us truly felt as well—he would miss him.

"LTGEN Wagner told his story from the soldier's viewpoint. He mentioned the names of all the brass and some of the elder statesmen. He served under Wayne and said that "Wayne was the father of America's special operations..." He left a standard that all had to measure up to. Many project and operations were planned and invariable, someone would say—"How would General Downing have done it...?"

"As we started filing out of the church, three volleys were heard. A bugler played the sweet, sad notes of Taps from the entrance as the soldiers loaded his casket into the hearse. Afterwards, the crowd surged around Kathy as literally hundreds tried to comfort her. A C-130 roared overhead in a fly-by to end the ceremony at the church.

"Finally, the family climbed into white limos and slowly drove behind a police escort to the reception. Lots of people stood on street corners or watched from their porches as the procession filed past. Police and State police blocked all the roads—lots of town people taking care of one of their home town guys. He was their hero, and ours, being laid to eternal rest.

"The reception was held at the Peoria Country Club on the bluffs above the Illinois River. The large building with rambling terraces and rooms up and down stairs hosted the many hundreds that came. Good food was piled on tables, many tales about Wayne heard from the groups that milled about the cookies and shrimp and roast beef sandwiches. Brian Williams, Lisa Meyers, and the rest of the NBC contingent of twelve stayed throughout the reception, and were genuinely interested in relaying their regard for and affection for Wayne.

"At 2 o'clock, we loaded up and headed for the airport. Good conversations and we were back on the ground at Dulles by 5:30 EST. We were all very thankful to Jim Kimsey for flying us out there. A moving ceremony—many stories told—and a great man, patriot, soldier, and family man was given a terrific send off. He will receive many military honors at West Point and I am sure the US Marines guarding the halls of heaven will welcome him as he arrives at Pearly Gates. He will be buried at West Point on Sept 27. That is the first of a three day reunion weekend for our class—many of us will attend the early burial before the reunion begins.

"Emerson wrote...'When nature takes from us an individual such as this, we immediately look to the horizon for a successor. But there is none...and none will come. For his class is extinguished with him...'"

"We classmates and company mates will miss him...Be Thou at Peace!"

Eulogy Notes—
Spalding/Academy of Our Lady Website

The following comments were posted on our class of 1958 (58er) website by Wayne's former classmates:

Susie Clark - Jul 21, 2007

"Ken and I went to Wayne's funeral, this morning . . at Saint Thomas and I must say I was in awe . . . . four full rows of West Point Grads . . representatives of every branch of service . . . Army Generals . . . too many to mention . . . Ross Perot gave the first eulogy . . . . Bryan Williams (NBC . . . he and Wayne went to Iraq together in early spring) . . . lots of 58ers . . . (thank you Jerry Cushing for talking me into going) we had great seats (thanks to Marilyn and Gordon . . and Ken and I) Good music . . a gun salute and a "flyover" . . . VERY PATRIOTIC . . . . and VERY CATHOLIC . . . . even some Latin music . . I am so glad I went."

Mary Ann Asciutto - Jul 21, 2007

Thanks, Susie, for sharing this with those of us that couldn't be there.

Dick Martin - Jul 21, 2007

"Susie,

Many Thanks for the report. Certainly sounded like it was impressive, as well it should have been. You didn't mention it so I'll ask: How is Kathy holding up?

Once again, thanks. Dick Martin"

Gordon Cundiff - Jul 22, 2007

"Thanks Susie, for capturing so well the feelings of Wayne's funeral. Let me also add my personal thoughts and impressions. The patriotic fever was indeed inspiring from start to finish and the powerful, thundering presence of the MC-130 Hercules that flew a mere few hundred feet over our heads as we exited the church with the paratrooper door open symbolized for me, both Wayne's escort home, but also the presence of you other 58ers (that could not be with us) dropping into the scene. The personal touch of three strong women in Wayne's life, first his mother Eileen (it is obvious where his steel courage came from), then his sister Marlianne, (his first Army of One that he ordered around) and Kathy, showing the strength (to be expected from a 58er) in her special way. Then on a spiritual note, Father Taylor gave an excellent homily, touching on Wayne's (and our) other source of strength, our relationship with God. He mentioned Wayne's changed, new "chain of command," and his "reunion" with his father & other sister. Fellow 58ers, I've been able (or found it necessary through business) to attend many, many funerals (including that of my parents, sister and grandparents) and I don't recall being touched any deeper than this funeral service. Please read the PJS newspaper accounts on www.pjstar.com. G."

Helen Wade – Jul 22, 2007
"Gordon, I couldn't agree with you more. I spoke with Fr. Taylor this morning before mass and told him thank you. He said having been a chaplain, he felt a real connection for where Wayne had been and what he'd done. I will never forget the MC–130 flyover and it's meaningful presence. Helen"

Terry McGrath – Jul 22, 2007
"Along with the PJS site, Gordon mentioned, WEEK TV's site has video coverage of the funeral. The Combating Terrorism School at West Point site has photo's of Wayne at varous stages of his career. It is a sad time but we were privileged to have known Wayne."

Joe Armentrout – Jul 23, 2007
"Your right Gordon, Susie did indeed capture the feelings of Wayne's funeral. It made me so very proud to be and American, in this very Christian country knowing we have people that learned from Wayne, still in command of our military. Our prayers for his mother Eileen, his sister and Kathy, are being joined by many, to help overcome such a loss for all."

Leo Hoerdemann – Jul 22, 2007
"We are fortunate as 58ers to have known Wayne; he touched us all in many ways. My deepest sympathy to Kathy & her family."

Bob Pfeifer - Jul 23, 2007

"Thanks to you Susie, for your personal description of General Downing's funeral. I read the news report in the Journal Star, but find the accounts of you and other 58ers more meaningful - more appropriate, more sensitive, more tangible. Thanks to you, Gordon Cundiff, Helen Wade, and other 58ers for helping the out-of-towners experience at least a fragment of the solemnity of the funeral. Bob P."

Terry Abercrombie - Jul 25, 2007

"Wayne's funeral was absolutely awesome! At first I was upset that I didn't get a seat in the main part of the church. However, the viewing screen at the back of the church was much larger than life and was especially helpful when it came time for the eulogies. I had a wonderful view as they carried the casket out and did the volleys.

I was really touched when the Schola from the cathedral sang *Ave Maria*, *Panis Angelicus* and *God Bless America*. During the service I kept wondering what I was doing there with all of the dignitaries that were present. Had they really come to pay respects to the same man that I was paying respects to? It was hard to fathom the Wayne Downing that took me to my first dance, with the General Wayne Downing that rose to such heights. When he came to our class reunions he was the same good-looking, popular Wayne he'd always been. He never seemed to put on airs or let you think that he was so important. Now I know that that is what made him so special. It was pure joy just being in his presence.

"Hebrews 13:2 says: "Don't forget to be kind to strangers, for some who have done this have entertained angels without realizing it." After listening to all of the wonderful eulogies, I must conclude that God put a mighty angel in our midst to be our friend and guard us, but now he's doing it from a much different vantage point. Hey Wayne, how's the view? See you later. Terry Hickey Abercrombie"

Dick Martin - Jul 26, 2007

"Terry, great commentary. It brought me back down to earth after a somewhat difficult time with Wayne's passing. Never thought that it would affect me so much, but I have a better understanding now as to why, thanks to the words from Hebrews 13:2 which I will again quote here saying: "Don't forget to be kind to strangers, for some who have done this have entertained angels without realizing it." It struck a chord. Thanks again. Dick Martin"

The Trip to the Burial Service at West Point

Tuesday, September 25, 2007—the first leg of the trip

I only had four hours of sleep and woke up with a bad headache. I picked up J.J. Heinz at his daughter Jackie's house in Morton about 6:50 a.m. We headed for Medaryville, Indiana to Jerry Cushing's farm where he and John Zeitz were waiting for us. The trip to Indiana went smoothly until after we got into Indiana and close to the farm—when we'd left the main routes. We had to turn onto 900 N or 400 W etc. There were no regular street names. We ended up traveling for 5½ hours instead of the normal 3½ hours to get to Jerry's.

Overnight stay—**Tuesday evening**

We stayed at the Comfort Inn & Suites in Austintown, Ohio. We checked in and took our luggage up to our designated rooms (each of the guys got their own room also), then went to the Quaker Steak & Lube for dinner. That was a really neat place to go. It was a Nascar-themed restaurant. There were rows of oilcans and other racecar memorabilia lining the walls.

Departure for West Point—Wednesday morning

We had a specific place we would all meet the next morning to continue our jaunt.

Pennsylvania and Ohio were beautiful and had so many eagles or red-tailed hawks that I couldn't count all of them. They were flying so high it was hard to distinguish what type of bird they were exactly. The trees had already started to put on their fall colors. Going through the mountains with the many hues just took my breath away.

Arrival—Wednesday afternoon

We arrived at Newburgh, New York around 3:00 or 4:00 p.m. and checked in at the Ramada. Then we set out for West Point to make sure where we needed to be the next morning and what time we could get inside the complex. The guards at the gate were very helpful.

As we were driving around Newburgh after leaving the West Point grounds, John had noticed some nice eating-places on the Hudson, so we went back there for dinner. We decided on Torches on the Hudson. What a fabulous place that was! They had a giant fish tank inside that ran the whole length of the bar with beautiful, colorful fish swimming inside. We could eat inside or right by the edge of the water and we chose the latter. There were boats docked close by. They had torches spaced along the edge that lit up the area so well that we had no trouble seeing the menu or what we were eating. The blackened swordfish with garlic butter was fabulous

The Burial Service at West Point, N. Y.

Thursday, September 27, 2007

We arrived at West Point at 11:00 a.m. It is simply gorgeous tucked in the mountains by the Hudson. It was built around 1802. Because we arrived early we were able to drive around West Point before the crowds of people arrived and we observed the soldiers getting the sleek and shiny horses from Arlington ready for the funeral procession. We weren't supposed to get out of our car so we were unable to get real close to take photos.

The Cadet chapel—the Catholic chapel was too small—where the burial service took place had a gigantic ceiling, awesome stained glass windows and quite imposing pillars. There was a cross at the center of the altar with a beautiful statue of a warrior standing in front of the cross. Each pew had kneelers for people to kneel if they chose to.

There was an ornate spiral staircase leading downstairs to the restrooms and the dressing room area where the military put on their uniforms. I felt like I was in a castle that I'd read about in books or seen in the movies. The view from the windows on the staircase was just as spectacular exposing the treetops. They also had a patio outside the lower level by the dressing area where people were mingling. While I was taking photos, the different military people started arriving carrying their uniforms.

Outside the front entrance of the Cadet chapel was a neat landing area breaking up the steps where quite a few people mingled that arrived early. The view was spectacular from there also. I was able to freely take photos there. Some of the men in civilian suits looked like military people with their large shoulders and massive physiques. There were steps and hills everywhere on the campus of West Point.

When the people in charge finally arrived to give us our places to sit, we were seated in the front half of the chapel closer to the altar than the middle. The West Point class of 1962—Wayne's class, that were having their 45th reunion that weekend—were seated starting with the row right behind us. There were 200 people in that group.

Wayne's West Point classmates made us feel very much like we were part of their group as well. We had a wonderful time talking to them and sharing stories back and forth about Wayne.

We heard many stories that weren't told at the podium. One man I talked to told me about Wayne helping him out when he was having difficulties. He didn't say what it was, but I got the impression it might have been something personal. This man acted like he was ready to cry when he was talking to me about it. It was so touching that tears welled up in my own eyes as well.

Even though they didn't have a catholic mass Reverend Thomas Taylor from Saint Thomas the Apostle Catholic Church in Peoria Heights performed the ceremony and gave the homily—He also participated at the memorial service on July 21 that took place in Peoria. Wayne's oldest daughter, Liz, gave a wonderful heart-warming talk. She had most of the people there crying including me. Tom Brokaw spoke next.

After the service there was a procession to the cemetery with the hearse, the caisson from Arlington, the rider-less horse, the West Point Band, representatives from all four branches of the service, the family, the dignitaries, the NBC news team, Wayne's West Point classmates from the class of 1962, other soldiers he served with and friends from the Spalding/AOL class of 1958 in Peoria. It was a mile walk from the Cadet chapel to the burial site, so some of us rode the bus. There was a stop at the Catholic chapel, where the Ranger guard removed Wayne's casket from the hearse and transported it to the caisson for the last leg of the procession to the gravesite.

The reception after the ceremony was held at the Thayer Hotel inside West Point, overlooking the Hudson, where the view was spectacular. Many people mingled outdoors on the surrounding veranda of the hotel.

Reflecting on the back to school dance from 1954, how did this mild-mannered boy that took me to my first dance in high school, become world-renowned? I'd have to say that it started with his wonderful upbringing from a widowed (since 1945) mother, Eileen Downing, who did everything in her power to give her children every opportunity to be successful. She did her job well. As for me—I have a special memory of Wayne, the young boy that I will cherish forever. Hey Wayne, save a dance for me.

Brian McEnany—USMA Class of '62—Eulogy (with assistance from Bob Meceda and Don Kauer)

Cadet Chapel, West Point, September 27
(posted on USMA website-used with permission)

"The Cadet Chapel was jammed. The lower panels in the high, stained glass panels were open, but not enough to clear the air. Generals and ex-generals filled the front pews behind Wayne's family. General McCaffrey (now an NBC news analyst) passed by along with the Superintendent, the Commandant, and the Dean. The NBC news team– Brian Williams, Lisa Meyers, Anne Curry and the video crews that had gone to Iraq with General Downing were all there to pay tribute to a fallen hero and friend. Representatives from each of the Special Operations Commands were present. Most were in civilian clothes– the varied uniforms from the memorial service in Peoria were not as evident this time.

"The Class of '62 and their wives filled almost half of the Chapel. We had come by car, bus and train from various states to attend reunion activities that were put on hold for the day. We arrived and parked at the Cavalry Plain and caught the buses to the Chapel. Wayne's old tactical officer – LTGEN (R) Richard Trefry and his wife Jacque - sat behind us. His old cadet company (H-2) was well represented. Talk of cadet days flowed back and forth across the pews until the organ began playing as the clock reached two o'clock.

"The commands of the honor guard were muffled by the granite walls of the chapel, but we could hear ruffles and flourishes played by the West Point band. The US Army honor guard from Washington brought the casket to the church door where it was then carried to the front of the Chapel by the Ranger honor guard. Prayers and hymns were said and sung – then the eulogies began. Jim Kimsey ('62) gave the first one, ending by paying tribute to the loss of his best friend. Jim Heldman ('62) talked about Wayne as a cadet and roommate – "Wayne was unique and never caught." Keith Hightower, a fellow Special Ops comrade, talked about Wayne as a soldier and the respect and honor shown him as the father of the modern Rangers. Wayne's daughter, Liz, spoke from the heart and in a choked, emotion filled voice, told us about her Dad and what his loss meant to her and her children. Tom

Brokaw (the ex-NBC news anchor) gave us a well-crafted account of Wayne as correspondent and advisor to NBC news, putting into words what many of us remembered about Wayne and his career.

"The military took charge after the service ended. The Ranger honor guard carried his casket back to the front door, the tread of their boots echoing in the still air of the Chapel. The West Point band played ruffles and flourishes as the US Army honor guard then carried his casket to a hearse for the procession to the cemetery.

"A contingent of cadets in full dress gray over white – a brigade staff and First Classmen with their swords and reds sashes - stood ready to march. Wayne's four-star flag was carried behind the color guard from the Corps of Cadets. A contingent of Rangers, the band, the immediate family and honorary pall bearers and finally the rest of us, walked down the hill to the cemetery. The flag at Trophy Point was at half-mast and hung limply in the humid air. When we turned the corner toward the cemetery – a slight breeze made the mile long walk a little easier.

"The procession halted before the gates of the cemetery as the casket was transferred from the hearse to a horse drawn caisson for the trip to the gravesite. We followed the military procession past the Old Chapel and around the care-taker's cottage. Just on the other side of the cottage, under the spreading arms of a giant oak, the final resting place for the general had been prepared. The military contingents drew up in a semi-circle around a canvas canopy – the cadet honor guard, the Rangers, the flag details. The caisson and horses were soon led away, their tasks were finished.

"We crowded around the canopied area amidst the gravestones of past graduates to hear the final words. This time, the various representatives from the Special Operations commands added their thoughts about Wayne's dedication to the Army, to West Point, and to the country. Our prayers rose skyward under the direction of the chaplain. The flag draped over his casket was carefully folded by the honor guard.

"Commands rang out! For the first time, I saw the arms of my classmates raised in hand salutes – not the cover your heart gesture that so many of us have done at Arlington – but an Army salute in respect for a fallen warrior' and classmate. The cadet sabers snapped up and down, the Rangers saluted - ribbons from tens of secret campaigns emblazoned on their crisp, green uniforms. An artillery battery fired 17 guns, the measured blasts echoing off the hillsides around us. A squad of Rangers fired three precise volleys into the air. The bugler played Taps – its mournful notes flowed across the gravesite and down the hillside to the river. Emotions rose within many of us and lots of handkerchiefs were pulled from pockets when the music died away. Just as the bugler finished playing, a strong breeze blew across the gravesite as if Wayne's spirit was anxious to be lifted away.

"A reception was held at the Hotel Thayer after the services and we made our way to its terraces and ballroom where discussions about Wayne continued. We shook hands with the NBC news crew. Brian Williams soon left to broadcast "The Evening News" from West Point that night. He added a short memorial segment at the end about the passing of a warrior. We had a chance to talk with members of Wayne's family – his mother and sister told us tales about how they always kept Wayne in his place even when he arrived in Peoria with his Secret Service detail. His sister made sure we knew that she was better in math than Wayne. Kathy Downing, surrounded by so many people, graciously accepted all the condolences.

"The mountains surrounding the Academy looked down on the scene below as they have for two hundred years or more. The river below flowed past serenely quiet. A train on the far bank wound its way through fields and forests. You could almost hear the strains of Benny Havens playing in the wind. I am sure that if Benny had lived during our time he would have known Wayne Downing. Nestled in the quiet of the Hudson Highlands, West Point had laid another member of the Long Gray Line to rest.

"The next morning, the Class of '62 returned to the Cadet Chapel for a class memorial service as we have done each reunion weekend. This time when the roll was read, Wayne A. Downing's name stood listed with our other 84 classmates honored that day.

"Be Thou at Peace!"

Mike Yap '67 shared on the website about Wayne's willingness to learn everything from the bottom up about the Science Applications International Corporation (SAIC) as an exceptional board member. "Wayne was the epitome of a warrior" said Mike.

Petition to rename the
Peoria International Airport

Wayne's Spalding/Academy (AOL) High School Class of 1958

One year after Wayne's death, our high school class of 1958 was trying to figure out what would be a good building that could be named after our former classmate four-star general Wayne Allan Downing. John David Heidewald had the idea of renaming the Peoria International Airport after him. Everyone agreed that it would be great to recognize Wayne in that way. Peoria Airport Authority already had some other names picked out. Wayne's name was not under consideration. They were going to make a decision soon. The groundbreaking was scheduled for October 10, 2008 at which time the new name would be announced. Heidewald drew up a petition to send to them to let them know that Wayne was deserving of having our airport named after him.

Petition LetterBy John David Heidewald—Wayne's Spalding/AOL Class of '58 used with permission

"To: Peoria Airport Board of Directors

"General Wayne A. Downing was born and raised in Peoria. He went on to West Point and rose through the ranks to four-star general available rank and the highest of any native Peorian, ever. (John Shaliskasvili immigrated to Peoria from Poland when he was sixteen and was also a four-star general).

"We believe that incorporating his name into that of the new Peoria Airport such as "General Downing International Airport at Peoria, Illinois" would be a decorous act for him and Peoria.

"Below are listed some significant facts about General Downing

- Place of birth Peoria, Illinois
- Allegiance United States of America
- Service/branch United States Army
- Years of service 1962-1996
- Rank General

- Commands held United States Special Operations Command
- U.S. Army Special Operations Command
- Joint Special Operations Command
- 75th Ranger Regiment
- Battles/wars Vietnam War
- Awards Defense Distinguished Service Medal (2)
- Distinguished Service Medal (2)
- Silver Star (2)
- Defense Superior Service Medal
- Legion of Merit (4)
- Soldier's Medal
- Bronze Star (7)
- Purple Heart
- military analyst, NBC News
- Significantly, General Downing chose to return to Peoria after his retirement until his death in July 2007

"We endorse the General Downing Airport At Peoria Petition to Peoria Airport Board of Directors."
531 Total Signatures
Sincerely,

The Undersigned

"I have read the General Downing Airport At Peoria Petition to Peoria Airport Board of Directors, and I hereby sign the petition:
Comments from a few people who signed the petition:

- **469. Paul F Bayless Jr.** "Served under Gen. Downing in the Special Operations community in the early 1990's."
- **468. Ranger Gary Strout** "Shadow Warriors, step out of the shadows for just a moment. Recall what this great man "Our Brother" sacrificed for America. No greater man deserves this Honor. No one knows better than we who served in the Special Operations community. God Bless all who support and sign this petition."
- **483. Nancy Rogers** "I am not personally involved in this ~ but I have this opinoion that important places should be named for people ~ not huge corporations. Sooner or later most people

find out a bit about the person such a place is named for and the achievements of that person have yet another chance to influence someone for the better. I wish you wisdom in your name selection."

Spalding/AOL website
Categories: General Wayne Downing in the news:

John Heidewald

"I called Ross Perot this morning and was asked to send the following email explaining our plans.

"Dear Mr. Perot, General Wayne Downing was a high school classmate and friend of mine. His mother, Eileen and his wife, Kathy both suggested that we request your help on our plan to name the new Peoria, IL airport in his honor.

"First, we would like to get your name and appropriate comments on our petition.

"Second, a letter or phone call to the board of directors of the airport authority would be appreciated. If this is acceptable, please call or email me at heidewaldj@gmail.com 727 595 6464. for the phone number and address to be called/addressed.

The URL for the petition is as follows:
http://www.PetitionOnline.com/general/petition.html
Please clik on this to see the petition and current signatures.
I anxiously await the addition of your name.

Thank you for your support,

John David Heidewald

It does look like some decisions will be made soon."

Read what others had to say:
John Zeitz - Aug 22, 2008 Viewers | Reply to this item

Heidi, Good move. I am trying to get in touch with Gary Stella, one of the Peoria County Airport authority board members. Gary Stella is a 70-71 year old former Cathedral grade school acquitance from 50+ years ago he is now active in several county boards including the Airport Authority. If anyone else from St Thomas (he now lives onprospect and works in the Heights) or the Cathedral knows Gary Stella, please fill me in. his cell is 309-253-7955.

Gordon Cundiff - Aug 22, 2008 Viewers | Reply to this item

Heide, another board member, Larry Stranz, is to call me back this afternoon. He will help us. I am also trying to reach Mike Landwirth. When you speak to Ross refer to the great job he did when he spoke at Wayne's funeral. CD/G

H. Ross Perot signed our petition and also sent a letter to the airport commission. Some quotes from his letter are as follows:

"General Downing is admired and respected by all who know and have served with him.
"General Downing is considered the Father of the Modern Rangers.
"General Downing served as Chairman and Founder of the Combating Terrorism Center at the U. S. Military Academy.
"The best test of a man's character is what he does for people who can do nothing for him.
"Throughout his life, General Downing has lived these words from Isaiah: Who will go?
"Send me!
"He has also lived these words: When principle is involved, be deaf to expediency.
"General Downing would be honored to have the Peoria Airport named in his honor and he richly deserves this tribute.

Ross Perot"

Spalding/AOL Class of 1958 website responses to Ross Perot's letter to the airport authority:

John Zeitz - Aug 22, 2008
"Fantastic!!!. It is wonderful that Mr. Perot has the time and energy to send a powerful account of Wayne's life. Hopefully our classmates will be motivated by this to make a final push for the

cause by signing the petition and having their friends and family sign the petition by Monday."

Joe Armentrout - Aug 23, 2008

"Fantastic does say it all John. Ross Perot was a great friend of the General, & it is great to have his name behind our petition. Thanks Heide, for sharing Ross Perot letter with us & I agree with John, it should be a great motivater for all of us."

Tom O'Brien - Aug 23, 2008

"John David: Keep up the good effort. Mary Ann and I are traveling this week and the old laptop is crankey at times. I check in when I can. YOU THE MAN Truck"

Terry Abercrombie - Aug 23, 2008

"Heide, what better friend could Wayne have than you? Just knowing how hard you've fought to get the Peoria Airport Authority to change the name of the airport says a lot for your dedication to your friendship. Just remember Matt 19:26 (paraphrased) "All things are possible to those who love the Lord and are fitting into His plan." Personally, I do pray that it's God's will that we get the name changed, though. If it doesn't happen, I feel there must be something better out there that we can get named after our famous classmate, Four-Star General Wayne Downing. You're doing everything you can to make it happen. In Olympic jargon I'll give you a perfect 10. Thanks, Heide."

John Heidewald - Aug 23, 2008

"Thanks for your kind comments, Terry, but I am going to stay with the airport deal. Anything else is for someone else to promote."

Bob Pfeifer - Aug 27, 2008

"Wow! Bob P."

Airport Groundbreaking Ceremony

On October 10, 2008 the groundbreaking ceremony for the new Peoria International Airport (PIA) passenger terminal and dedication to General Wayne Allan Downing went off as planned. I think we owe a lot of praise for Ross Perot's support. Things really started rolling once his name was on our petition and he sent that wonderful letter. Ross Perot came to Peoria for the groundbreaking. What a celebration it was for our Spalding/AOL class of 1958. The new name of our airport—Wayne A Downing Peoria International Airport—is at last a reality. What a wonderful sound in that name.

Comments from the Spalding/AOL website:

Gordon Cundiff - Oct 10, 2008 View | Viewers

Twenty lookers yesterday on the website, but only two talkers (posters), today will be a bigger news day. See you at the airport. Someone said that (for VIP) it was by invitation only, but they do not know the class of 58. We will be there with or without invites. Let them try to stop us. We are MIP, most important people, at least to each other. G/CD

Terry Quigley - Oct 10, 2008 Viewers | Reply to this item
I hope there was a good turn out.
Sorry I could not be in attendece
Gordon Cundiff - Oct 10, 2008 Viewers | Reply to this item

It was a great turn out of 58ers for a most impressive program. All of our classmates should be very proud of our famous classmate General Wayne. Wayne's mother was tributed by several speakers for raising such a fine man who served our Country so well. Mrs. Downing, Marlianne and Kathy were all justly proud. Tomorrow's PJS will have front page coverage. When Ross Perot was speaking I couldn't help but vividly recall a conversation I had with Wayne about twenty years ago at his niece's wedding when Wayne spoke very highly of Ross who was running for President about that time. Today, Ross returned the favor to Wayne, in a most profound way. G/CD

Joe Armentrout - Oct 14, 2008 Viewers | Reply to this item

CD/ I agree of course with everything you have said regarding the dedication of the Peoria Airport and it's real "New Name ! General Wayne A. Downing~Peoria International Airport,"~ "John David should be very, very, proud, of his tremendous work and imput to have this happen! I still marvel that it took a "now", out of towner to direct all of us ~ that live here, what needed to be done! "Thanks John David "~what a great deed you have accomplished for the Downing Family, the 58er class,~ The Rangers. and the list goes on! Yes, you had some great help, but only after YOU started the ball rolling!

Joe Armentrout

Thanks JDH
Sue&joe

John Zeitz - Oct 14, 2008

Joe: Well stated.

Gordon Cundiff - Oct 15, 2008

Everyone knows where the credit goes, but John does not seek the recognition. Do you think that is why he skipped out of the Country? Thanks to him anyway. G/CD

Tom O'Brien - Oct 15, 2008

Last night on NBC Nightly News Brian Williams did a nice piece on the dedication. You can see the video if you go to the NBC news site. http://www.msnbc.msn.com/id/3032619/ Truck

Terry Rafool - Oct 16, 2008

Thanks Tom/Truck - what a tribute. Such a legacy. Stay well one and all. Terry R

John Zeitz - Oct 16, 2008

Thanks for the info Truck: the link worked fine-- It is one of the last stories in the 37 news clips on file. A very nice tribute to General Wayne.

The Spalding/AOL class of 1958 had a reunion in 2010 coinciding with the dedication of a six feet high bronze statue (paid for by Ross Perot) of General Downing at the entrance to the airport. It is very impressive and Our class is very happy and appreciative that Mr. Perot honored his friend Wayne Downing in another monumental way.

Angel Sculpture-*computer-enhanced*

Glory

Some people are such a pleasure to know
Quietly doing nice things—not for show.
They seem to do it with joy in their heart
I'm thankful that I got t'know one small part.

Of a sweet woman—an angel at best—
That God is putting her still thru the test.
She is still earning her wings here on earth
Where heaven bound she will win a prime berth.

What do I wish for an angel so rare?
God will enfold her in all of His care
Till it's time for an angel's new story
She'll be content in all of her glory.

Eileen Downing

Downing really took parenting seriously and did everything in her power so her three children would succeed. She didn't think much about getting married again, because that might have gotten in the way of her child rearing. When Wayne was in high school, she was involved in the Mother's Club. Downing would have the kids listen to classical music, close their eyes and let their imaginations take over. She told me that she was a tough mother.

Eileen Downing is ninety years young and with a remarkable memory. She still lives on her own in a condo. What a wonderful sense of humor Downing has—she laughs at herself a lot—and a great personality, that was also evident in her three children who are all deceased now. Her youngest daughter, Becky Downing (Terry) Hartnett died when she was 47, Wayne, the oldest died in 2007 at the age of 67 and Marlianne Downing (J. Michael) Fortune died a year later, in 2008 when she was 67 years old.

Angels to Guard You

(For Chief Master Sergeant Nancy Geisler USAF, retired)

I pray that angels from above
Surround you in God's holy love
And be with you in that far place
Enfolding you in loving grace.

When duty calls you far from home
Angels will be where'er you roam.
I know you have a job to do
Just know that angels follow you.

What matters most in this great life
Doing the job without the strife
And knowing what is right and good
Protecting all our brotherhood.

We are blessed. There's no grander place
Or greater example of the human race.
So do your job then hurry back
From that war-torn country called Iraq.

That Kind of Man

(For Staff Sergeant Mark Faginkrantz, retired and former President
George W Bush) Operation Enduring Freedom 2003

I pray that angels from above
Surround you in God's holy love.
And go with you to that far place
Enfolding you in loving grace.

I know you'll do your job quite well.
You'd never waiver. I can tell.
So go out there. Do what you can;
For you are just that kind of man.

What matters most when life is o'er,
Is knowing how to keep the score
On what is right and what is good
In guarding all our brotherhood.

We are blest. There's no grander place
Or greater example of the human race.
So go out there. Do what you can;
For you are just that kind of man.

TRIBULATION

The Mystery of the Rose

The rose is a reminder
Of what Our Lord can do
Amid the wind and rainy days
The clouds across the blue.

It starts just as a tiny seed
With sun and rain and soil
Nurtured by His loving hands
Each seed is sown thru toil.

Then the bud unfolds to form
A regal sight to see
Each petal laying side-by-side
Opening up in majesty.

The thorns that rest along each stem
Remind me of that day
When Jesus wore the crown of thorns
To wash our sins away.

So when the storms in life appear
Just know that others care
And look up toward the heavens above
You just might see a rainbow there.

The Encounter

I used to work at Caterpillar Tractor Company (Cat). I started putting service manuals together at the Boggus Building on Washington Street in Peoria, Illinois in 1959. While I was on maternity leave with my first baby, Chuckie I was laid off—from 1960-1962.

I was called back to Cat at the Morton, Illinois plant in 1962 to second shift. I spent my first year in Morton as a messenger riding a bike throughout the plant, from the main office to the shipping and receiving offices out in the shop. I got divorced about three months after I started work at Morton. In 1963 I was promoted to keypunch operator. I loved my job as a keypunch operator, quickly getting into making my own programs for the keypunch machine. Most of our work had to be verified, but the computer programmers (system analysts) were on a tight schedule—taking turns on the mainframe computer—so they didn't have time to wait for the work to be verified. I was a very accurate typist, so I did most of the keypunching for the programmers. I found a lot of mistakes, so that was advantageous to them also. The computer language was fascinating and I got to where I knew what they wanted, even when they forgot to write it down. It was just common sense to me. If they put down an opening parenthesis, I knew that they needed a closing parenthesis also. I'd see where they forgot periods at the end of the programs, plus many other things.

I worked second shift for three or four years. There was little time for me to meet or date anyone. Most people had daytime jobs. It was a very lonely time in my life. Around 1965 or 1966 I was transferred to first shift doing the same job.

One Sunday in February of 1968—after being divorced for six years—I went to a Caterpillar retirement dinner held at the Green Gables restaurant and bar on old route 150 in East Peoria. I loved the cozy, downhome atmosphere of that place. That's when I met Larry Abercrombie. He was at the dinner with a co-worker. They sat across the table from my six-year old son, Chuck Perry and me. Larry kidded around with Chuck most of the day. I thought he must really like kids and of course Chuck loved every minute of the special attention he was getting from Larry.

The next Friday someone from work asked me to go to Green Gables after work. I agreed to go, recalling the fun at the dinner the Sunday before. It ended up that Larry showed up and he asked me for a date. I told him I didn't think that was a good idea, because he was dating a co-worker. Larry said it was never serious, but I had to talk to my co-worker first and see how serious she was about Larry. She said it wasn't serious and if I wanted to go out with him, go ahead. We fell in love right away. He was such an easy going and happy person. He just swept me off my feet.

I had a car that wouldn't start quite frequently, causing me to be late for work many times. There was a gas station one block away, but there was no one to come and start my car as early as I needed them. Work started at 7:18 a.m. and the other men at the gas station didn't get to work until 8:00 a.m. None of the mechanics could find out the exact problem with my car. My boss, Burl Shelor (deceased) didn't believe that there was something wrong with my car. He thought I just overslept. One day I actually did oversleep and Shelor called me and said I had to take three days off without pay for being late. I was really upset. I needed every penny I made. My boss was married and kept trying to get me to go out with him and I said I wouldn't go out with a married man. In reality I would not have gone out with him even if he were single, because he seemed to be a womanizer. I suspected that there was more to the three days off than me just being late and maybe part of it was because I wouldn't go out with him.

Shelor was always kidding around with me at work and I would think that the other women could tell that he liked me and probably thought I actually did go out with him. It was mostly women that I worked with. When Larry found out about what my boss did he said, "Why don't you quit work and marry me?" I was thrilled to death. I truly loved Larry and he got along so well with Chuck, that I thought he would be a good choice for a husband. It was important to me that whoever I married get along well with my eight-year old son Chuck as well.

I didn't tell my boss I quit. I did tell his assistant, who was my best friend, Dixie Glasford. When the three days were up, I went in to personnel and talked to the personnel manager. He asked me why I was quitting so I told him. He said I should have told him sooner. He said that Caterpillar frowns on bosses that ask the employees out and especially when they're married. I thought they would stick up for my boss—not me. Dixie said that Shelor had a large project he was saving for me when I went back to work. A lot of women didn't like to do the hard jobs, but I loved the challenge of it. I had a hard time sitting for very long at a time even back then. When I got engrossed in a difficult task it seemed to get my mind off my pain.

Larry was on strike with Illinois Bell Telephone Company—working with long distance communications—when we met. He started working there right after being discharged from the Navy. I admired the fact that he had gotten a part-time job right away tending bar at Green Gables until the strike was over. That showed to me that he wasn't afraid to work hard and would be a good provider.

After we were married Larry started driving my car and gave me his car to drive. My car had a bad choke on it. Larry put on a new choke and the car started well from then on. I couldn't believe all of those other mechanics couldn't spot that. I could have opened the choke myself when it wouldn't start if I had known that was what was wrong with it.

I was at one of my favorite fabric stores one day in 1969—I've been sewing and designing my own clothes since I was fourteen—when the owner asked me if I would model some of the clothes I made for a style show for the Christian Business and Professional Women's Club, that was going to meet at the Pére Marquette Hotel. I said I would do it. I'd never heard of that club, but I got a discount on the fabric I bought to make two new things for the style show. I made a long double knit evening dress of pale green with gold designs running through it, with a slit to the knee on one side, a mandarin collar and long sleeves. I made a small evening purse to match it and put a gold chain on it for the handle of the purse. I also made a black, double knit, three-quarter length pant coat.

Those of us in the style show were invited to stay for the dinner, but no one wanted to stay. I didn't either, but as I was leaving, the guest speaker started talking. I was enthralled by her message. There was a couch right outside the meeting room and I sat there and listened to the whole talk. The speaker shared her life story and told how she became a Christian—I was entranced with her witnessing.

The next day Dixie Glasford, my friend from Caterpillar called me. She saw me modeling in the style show. I told her how I was captivated with the speaker. She said that she would invite me to a dinner meeting the next time she went. She did just that and I started going every month. Soon after that, I was asked to be the decoration chairman and decorate the tables with a different theme every month. I agreed to do it.

Larry and I were so much in love and had an exceptional marriage for 3½ years. We had everything going for us, a lovely home surrounded by woods, thirty-two hickory trees in our immediate yard area, in a secluded spot with only eight houses near us. I could look out the floor-to-ceiling window in the living room and watch the luminous sunset through the trees and an equally pleasing sight watching all of the wonderful birds in the daytime and the moonrise at dusk out our dining room window at the back of our house or while out on our patio. It was truly a sight to behold.

Besides my son Chuck, Larry and I had one son Curt who was three years old by now. Everything was going well. Then we found out I was going to have another baby. I was thrilled. When I was dating Larry I told him I wanted four or five kids. I came from a large family and it was natural for me to want more children. I didn't ask Larry how many kids he wanted and he didn't offer to tell me. Larry was not happy about the pregnancy. He didn't want to believe or accept it. We started growing apart. I had my last baby, Todd on December 2, 1972. It was a difficult pregnancy and birth. It took me nine months to get over the birth.

That same year Larry and his boss, Hank Wankel, were out of town on a service call with long distance communications in a town north of Peoria. Larry was checking long distance telephone lines when Wankel heard the sound of running water and decided to walk over to investigate a creek close by. He called Larry to come and see something. There was a deceased, nude girl lying in a ditch. We later found out that it was fifteen-year old Tracey McKewn. They reported it to the police right away. Larry didn't talk about it much after that day. I had no idea that it was bothering him.

One thing I didn't know at the time was the fact that Larry might have been an alcoholic. He drank and smoked quite a bit every day, the whole time we were married, except if he had a bad cold or the flu. Too much alcohol can be a depressant and the alcohol probably affected his coping skills. I rationalized that at least he wasn't drinking in a bar—he was home with me. My first husband was out in the bars quite a bit, but he wasn't drinking; he was gambling. That's why I didn't care if Larry drank at home.

The Stranger in the Parking Lot

In 1973—a year after my youngest son, Todd was born—I started a job at Carson, Pirie, Scott & Co in downtown Peoria selling sewing machines and teaching sewing lessons. I really enjoyed that job. One bitter cold January day in 1974—while at work—someone called in sick at the sewing machine department, at the other Carson's store at Northwoods Mall. My boss, Mrs. Exie Miller asked me if I could go to the mall and open the department. I quickly walked the one block to my car, which was parked at Eckwood Park, bordering the Illinois River. The wind chill was below zero and I was freezing. As I was leaving the parking lot a man walked up to the side of my car exposing himself. I was terrified. I watched out my rear view mirror to see if I could see what car he left in, but he lingered and I couldn't wait. I had to hurry to the mall. I was unable to get a license number. I called the police when I got to the mall. The policeman said I didn't need to worry about it and that I'd probably never see him again.

The next day I was leaving work and walking to my car with another Carson employee. She had just asked me about the incident the day before. I started describing what the man looked like. I said that he kind of looked like the man standing in the parking lot about thirty feet away from us. I no sooner said that that I discovered it was the same man and he was standing next to my car. (I can still picture that scene today). This time I was able to see his license number as he drove away. I made a mental note of it, then hurried home and called the police. When the police investigated the license number, they discovered that the number belonged to someone that lived by Chicago, and he didn't look anything like the man that I saw. We later found out that the man I saw at Eckwood Park had a fictitious license plate. The police department decided to have two detectives follow me to and from work for three days. Lucky for me the stranger never came back.

I was still scared. Had the man been watching me before? Did he know where I lived? Would he come back? Larry drifted farther away from me. He always had something he should be doing instead of spending time comforting me. I needed Larry so bad to help me get through that, but he wrapped himself more than ever into yard work or bookwork that he did at his desk in our bedroom.

The busier Larry got the more disenchanted I became with our marriage. He didn't want to take me anyplace when he got off work or on the weekends or even spend time with me. Larry took care of all the bills and rarely left me enough money to do anything while he was at work. I needed an escape to get away from my neighbor's four to six miniature schnauzers that barked most of the time. She had a dog business in her home. I chauffeured the boys to ball games, swimming, movies, etc. I listened to complaints when people called about our dog Snoopy getting loose. I cooked, cleaned house, made new clothes for the boys and Larry and everything else a mother and housewife should do. It didn't leave me much time for myself. Larry expected the house to be perfect all of the time. I saw that it was that way, but I felt like a slave.

I was selfish and didn't see Larry's way of thinking at all. I blamed him for all our difficulties. I kept telling myself how much I sacrificed for him, never once understanding all of the sacrifices he made for me. I think in reality that Larry and I worked so hard to please each other that we lost sight of ourselves. That was such a shame. Deep down I knew Who we needed in our lives. I begged him to go to counseling and to church, but he wouldn't go.

I finally decided that I couldn't put up with all the hardships anymore. I decided I'd rather be alone than be married to someone that didn't have any time for me. I told Larry I wanted a divorce. Even thinking about another divorce was devastating to me. Another divorce would mean another failure on my part. Catholics weren't supposed to get divorced.

Larry agreed to let me go to Florida for a week to think things out. I put the divorce on hold for a while. When I was in Florida Larry wrote me a beautiful Love Letter. Here is my precious Love Letter from Larry—unaltered—that he wrote to me while I was in Florida, in the summer of 1974:

The Love Letter

"My Sweetheart Terry,

"I have been composing this Love Letter all day. After talking to you tonight I almost decided not to write after all, but my Love for you is so very strong and deep that my own depression and slight disappointment will not stand in the way.

"As you know, I have difficulty in expressing myself in an easily understood manner and my spelling and handwriting is terrible, but at least you will know it is me doing the writing, altho it won't sound like me.

"Honey, I am so terribly, terribly sorry that I completely did not understand you and your needs during the past several years. I have loved you all that time in my own way, which I realize now was very selfish and very boyish, not like a truly loving and understanding husband should be. I am very sorry that it has made you very seriously considering divorce to finally get through to me and finally open my eyes. My poor loving Darling, you have tried to tell me so many times. I guess I didn't understand or didn't care to try to understand, I honestly don't know. I hear the expression between men that they say 'Women are funny (meaning odd).' Possibly I thought you are funny too. I now realize you are not *funny*. I am the one who is *funny*.

"You are a woman—all woman—with very much love to give. You are a woman who is very sensitive, who has many needs and desires that it takes a good and determined man to fulfill your needs. I am talking about in many ways. When a decision needs to be made, you want me to make it. I let you make it. Suppose you want me to come sit on the couch with you and maybe watch a TV program together, no, I have other things to do so I won't be with you. I finally come out and sit down. You want me to lean over and kiss you (not a peck, a kiss) and tell you *I love you*. You want me to sit close and put my arm around you. You just want my love and affection and tenderness and be reassured of my love for you. You want to talk to me, to unload your problems and troubles to me, to tell me of the enjoyable things that have happened during the day, to tell me of the things you'd like to do in the future with me and with the kids and with other people and with other things and items, (sewing, the house, etc.). No, what do I do? I drag a can of beer in and glue my eyes and ears to the TV set!!!

"These are only two examples of your needs and desires and we both could see they are not at all hard to take care of.

"As I told you on the phone I finally went to sleep about 2 a.m. this morning and I am very tired but I want to write more tonight and then I'll write more at work. Please, Honey, believe me. I have been so ignorant. Oh God, I am so sorry. I love you so much. I can make it so much better. You have no way of knowing how much my eyes have opened and how my love for you has deepened.

"You know, there has been 2 or 3 times this week when I was trying to get you up in the morning, you poor Darling, you were trying so hard to get up. I looked at you and said to myself, 'You dumb fool. Look! There are thousands and thousands of men who would give their right arm for a woman like this. Buddy, you own this woman, she is yours. What have you done? You turned your back, you idiot! And to top it off, she loves you! She doesn't now, though, and why should she? Do you blame her? You could have taken care of her easily, but you didn't! You are lucky someone else hasn't moved in and taken over! Boy what a Boob you are!!!'

"Honey, what a dumb idiot I have been being married to you and never realizing the type of woman you are. It is 1:00 a.m. and I must stop now. I will add more to this Love Letter tomorrow. This is not a love letter as one would expect a love letter to be, but I am trying to explain myself to you about how I was, and now that I understand, how I am now. I sincerely hope that you abided by what I wrote on the envelope containing this letter rather than curiosity. I am so sorry and feel so badly that I didn't open my eyes long long ago. That guy in the parking lot back in January would not have any effect on you if I had done right by you.

"Tuesday, Noon

"Hi, Honey,

"I am eating lunch in the truck so please excuse any mustard or crumbs you may find. I feel so much better right now because I realized what you told me on the phone last night. (I am such a slow thinker). You said you wanted to come back and talk to me before giving me an answer. I took it that you wanted to say that to stay married I would have to do this and this, that and that and so forth. But no! You want to search out my feelings and my sincerity! You want more time!!!!!

Gosh, I have been frantically and desperately trying to reach out to you, to get through to you by a deadline. Time! Time! We have plenty of time to work things out. Please realize this. Forget a deadline. We have time. We can think much better with time.

"My thoughts are jumbling around today and it makes it difficult to write. I was going frantic this morning to finish this love letter until I realized that you were asking for more time to think about us. More time will make me write you a better letter. Please believe me. Everything I have said to you in the last 3 or 4 days about my eyes being open and my love for you is very true and very sincere.

"I just reread this letter just before starting to write again today and I don't particularly like it. However, every word in it is true and it is <u>my thoughts and feelings.</u> The only change I would make is the statement about the instructions on the envelope. I wrote it at 1:00 a.m. this morning and it is in poor taste. I was going to put on the envelope 'for you not to open it, just burn it up if you had made up your mind that you were definitely going to divorce me. Otherwise to please read the letter.' I was depressed last nite and didn't realize that you wanted more time, that there is still much hope for us.

"This event in our lives has been probably the best thing to ever happen to me. It has really opened me up to what life should be like. It has made me look inside myself. It has made me realize what Love really is. It has made me fall so much more deeper in Love with you, Honey. It has made me see what the special relationship there is between husband and wife. It made me see that you were giving me that special relationship but that I was not giving it to you. My poor Sweet Darling, you have been deprived and starved for a man's Love all your life. First no Father, then you could not get it in your first marriage, then you could not get it from me. Well, for the first time in your life you have finally found it and it is in me. For I have finally found myself. I will give you that special relationship that now exists with all the Love I have for you. And that love is so true and so very deep. My Poor Darling, I am so terribly sorry that this did not come to me so much sooner.

"I guess that by me not understanding what Love and marriage is all about I just took things for granted. I assumed that when a man took a wife she would bear him children, satisfy his desires, cook and wash and keep house in appreciation for being provided for. But that is not so, is it Honey? I see now. I understand now.

"I certainly hope that you are beginning to understand me and are beginning to believe that I truly Love you. I have great difficulty expressing myself and it is hard to get my words out so they are understood by someone else. It is very hard writing this letter, and believe me, I am not putting down words on paper. I am saying them to you as if you were right here beside me. And I sure wish you were.

"I will make all this up to you by being a good and deeply loving and understanding husband to you. It will be hard, but not very hard because you have always given your Love to me and I know you will continue to do so. Perhaps even more so than in the past. I will have to change myself in several ways but I can and will do it because I do Love you, Honey, and I want to do right by you.

"This has been a great emotional experience for me and to you also, but I am so emotionally overwhelmed. I feel so different. I see things so differently now. It is so completely overwhelming that I can't explain it to you.

"Honey, I have been trying to explain things all last week and I believe I finally began getting through to you Friday nite. I was very panicky though because you said you would make your decision in Florida. Now last night you said you wanted to return and talk to me first before making a decision. I now know you want more time and you want to know really how I feel about you. We will take time and talk. We can take all the time in the world. Perhaps I should take a couple of days off and you and I go somewhere together for a while and work things out. I know you are very hurt and very confused but with time we will make a go of things. I Love you so much.

"Well, Honey, I have just finished rereading this letter. It is not a good letter. I feel that I haven't convinced you that I do and want to Love you. But it is hard for me to put things in words. I have said about everything that I want to say in this letter. I see that I was thinking a little differently last night than today but everything in here I feel needs to be said to you. I certainly hope that this letter doesn't make things worse but I feel it will help make things better. I now will be very patient and wait for you to return home and to return to me.

"I so very much Love you, Honey. I mean that sincerely.

All my Love to you, Larry"

When I got back from Florida I decided to try really hard to work things out with him. Without God in our lives it was very difficult handling diversities. It was just too much for me. "A person standing alone can be attacked and defeated, but two can stand back-to-back and conquer. Three are even better, for a triple-braided cord is not easily broken." Ecclesiastes 4:12 NIV. Because God was the common denominator missing in our marriage, we were divorced on Halloween 1974. In retrospect, I think that if he hadn't been drinking so much, we wouldn't have gotten divorced. He was a wonderful guy and I genuinely and deeply loved him.

After our divorce my self-esteem plummeted even lower than it was before. How could this happen to me again?

The Rendezvous

It was Christmas 1976, two years after my divorce. The Christmas tree was all decked out with handmade ornaments my sons and I had fashioned—satin ones, wooden ones, lights and tinsel. On top of the tree was a Mr. and Mrs. Santa Claus decoration, with a blinking circle of lights on the perimeter that gave the tree its special personality. My three sons were so happy. Chuck was fifteen, Curt was almost eight and Todd was four. My boyfriend was also with us and in the Christmas spirit.

It all started two days before Christmas. I worked part time at Sears's department store selling women's clothing. That small job was all the income I had at the time. My boyfriend brought Curt and Todd into work to have supper with me. Todd started teasing me and ran away from me. He wouldn't come when I called for him so I went after him, picked him up and brought him back to join us. As I picked him up I got an excruciating pain in my lower abdomen. I didn't worry about it because I've been getting sharp pains like that occasionally for about three or four years. When I got one it stopped me dead in my tracks, but went away as quickly as it came.

I was used to being in a lot of pain since my auto accident when I was sixteen. I didn't tell Dr. Atherton about the current pain, because my previous doctor never believed me if I told him about any pain. He'd say it was stress or in my head; so I just kept it to myself. I wasn't too alarmed when the pain continued through Christmas Eve. I assumed it would leave eventually. I attributed the pain to the stress of getting ready for Christmas. Retail work at Christmas time is very hectic.

Christmas morning the boys rushed into my bedroom bursting with excitement. Curt said, "Mom! Mom, Santa was here. Come and see all the presents he left for us!" It was 6:15 a.m. and I had been up half the night trying to get all the last minute preparations done. I crawled out of bed with what little strength I could muster and lay down on the sofa to watch my happy sons unwrap their presents. Chuck got a tape player, Curt got a baseball and bat, and Todd got a big truck among other things. Curt and Todd helped me with my presents. I was too sick to really care.

Curt and Todd's dad came around 10:30 to take them to his house for more Christmas there and Chuck went with his dad. My boyfriend planned to stay all day with me. We had reservations for dinner at one of my favorite eating-places—a warm and cozy place called the Gold Lion Steakhouse located at the lower edge of Bradley Park.

As the morning progressed the pain worsened and I developed a fever. I knew I didn't have the flu, so I finally decided I'd better call Dr. Atherton. I didn't want to call him on Christmas, but I didn't know what else to do. He is the one doctor that said to call him no matter what time of day it was, if I really needed him and I surely did that particular Christmas day. I described the pain and told him where the location of the pain was and he told me to go to the emergency room at Methodist Hospital.

I don't like hospitals, but I would do anything to rid myself of the pain. I told my boyfriend, "They'll probably check me over and give me some medication. We should be back in time to make the dinner reservation."

The emergency room (ER) was so quiet I think I could have heard a whisper with no one in sight except the nurse at her station doing paper work. The slim ER doctor with a neatly trimmed mustache arrived, checked me over and sent me to the X-ray department. I was shocked when I was told what was wrong. He said, "You have a strangulated hernia and you can't leave the hospital until it is removed." I couldn't believe it! I said, "How could I possibly have a hernia?" He said, "It happens sometimes to women."

I cried quite a bit that day. I blamed God for all of this. How could He be a good God and let all these negative things happen to me? Everybody else was home with their families enjoying Christmas dinner and I was up in that miserable hospital room with an intravenous feeding for my dinner. Jokingly I told the nurse that I didn't like my turkey dinner at all. She laughed and said, "That was the best dinner I could find."

I called Larry and told him I had been admitted to the hospital. I asked him if he could keep the boys until I got home a week later. He said that was fine. I was operated on the Monday after Christmas.

Besides missing my sons for a week, I probably would miss an opportunity for a full-time position selling sewing machines; that I'd been promised as soon as the holidays were over. My recuperation would be for six weeks.

The week went by slowly and finally, on New Year's Eve I was released to go home. I was elated! I could see my boys soon—before Larry put them to bed—if I just hurried home. When I called Larry he said he wasn't bringing them back. He and his wife were going to keep them. He remarried nine months after our divorce. "How could this happen again?" My first husband, Bob took Chuck from me thirteen years ago when he was two years old. He left Chuck with some strangers that I didn't know. Bob finally called me after two weeks and told me where to go to pick Chuck up. When I picked Chuck up he was stuttering—he never did that before—and it didn't stop until Chuck was about twelve or thirteen.

I used to blame God for all of the bad things in my life and I took credit for the good things. In reality it was quite the opposite. The good things that happened to me came from God and the bad things were usually my own doing. God has a reason for everything. I didn't pray very often, but this day I prayed to God to help me. Deep down I knew that He was really the only One who could help me.

I called the police, but they were unable to help. I wished I had a lawyer to call, but who would be available on New Year's Eve anyway? I couldn't stand the thought of living without my boys. They meant everything to me. We've always been real close. I told Larry I was going to call his Grandmother and tell her what he'd done. His Grandmother Gladys and I remained very close even after our divorce. I would not have called her, but Larry thought I would. I persuaded Larry to bring them back. He brought Curt and Todd home within the hour. This event was the beginning of my wonderful journey with the Lord and I am so grateful that He died on the cross for me (and also for you). My life was forever changed; although it took me another six years to come to terms with Larry and our divorce. Later, in *The Awakening,* I talk more about my enlightenment.

When I returned to work from my medical leave, I got that full-time job I wanted selling sewing machines, which led into a position as a decorator consultant for that company—the most rewarding and interesting job I'd had up until then—selling custom draperies and re-upholstery.

"I waited patiently for the Lord; He turned to me and heard my cry. He lifted me out of the slimy pit, out of the mud and mire; He set my feet on a rock and gave me a firm place to stand. He put a new

106

song in my mouth, a hymn of praise to our God. Many will see and fear the Lord and put their trust in him."—Psalm 40:1-3 TLB. I can still relate very well to that bible verse. What a wonderful rendezvous that was—and the start of my Christian walk with My Lord and Savior, Jesus Christ.

Amazing Grace

At the next dinner meeting—after my operation—for the Christian Business and Professional Women's club, I confirmed my conversion when the speaker asked anyone who just turned their life over to Jesus Christ, she said to write your name on the back of your admission ticket and hand it to her at the end of the evening. I now knew without a doubt who those speakers were referring to—me. It was like I had been looking at the things in my life through a fuzzy lens. It's so amazing how God can turn a negative, depressing human being into a positive, happy and grateful Christian.

I didn't know that I wasn't a Christian until The Rendezvous. I tried to live a Godly life by volunteering and doing nice things for other people. I thought doing good works would get me to heaven. I prayed only when I wanted something.

I considered myself a religious person. I was baptized. I went to church. I sang in the choir. I donated my time for different causes. I was treasurer of the Girls Club and the Mixed Chorus (the choir and we put on a play in the fall every year for the employees) at different times when I worked at Caterpillar. I was the decoration chairman for the Peoria Christian Business and Professional Women's Club. I listened to the speakers for five years before I realized that the testimonies of the speakers told us how to invite Jesus Christ into our hearts, I could and should apply to my own life. I was very *hard of listening*.

I could relate well to the song, *Amazing Grace*. "…for I was lost, but now I'm found, was blind but now I see…" I was blinded by worldly things for a few years, but in all that time, God never lost sight of me. He always saw the good in me and was very patient in waiting for me to come back home to Him. I am and always will be forever grateful. God's grace is so amazing.

The Awakening

In 1982—eight years after Larry and I divorced—I finally owned up to my part in the demise of our marriage. It was true that Larry changed a lot, but what role did I play in his changes? Sometimes both people are at fault and maybe sometimes neither one is. Sometimes outside factors enter into it.

I called Larry one day and asked him if He would meet me at Lum's restaurant to talk. He agreed to meet me. I just had to tell him how sorry I was about blaming him for everything that went wrong in our marriage and that I was partly to blame for his changing, possibly. It was great to finally admit that, because Larry was a real nice guy—and he deserved to know my newfound idea about our divorce. If I had found the Love Letter sooner I probably would have tried to mend our relationship at the same time I apologized. Larry was so happy that I told him how I felt about our divorce. Even if he hadn't been, it was the right thing for me to do. My awakening was many years in coming, but I thank God that it came about.

Larry passed away on January 8, 2011. It was three months after his death that I discover his beautiful Love Letter written for me so many years ago. If Larry were still alive right now, I would have loved to go back and ask him to give me another chance. Now I'll have to wait until I get to heaven. Reading it now as a Christian, it sheds a new light on everything. It gives me much comfort and wonderful memories.

The Hiding Place

It was Thursday, July 19, 1984. Dr. David Johnson looked at my two big toes, then took my temperature—it was 100 degrees—and did blood tests. My temp is usually below the norm of 98.6. He sent me to St. Francis Hospital for x-rays and gave me a prescription for a five-day supply of Keflex (an antibiotic). If I didn't have any side effects he said to refill the med and to take it for three weeks. Dr. Johnson said, "You might have a bone infection. If the x-rays show that you do you'll have to be hospitalized for six weeks and take antibiotics for one year. Stay off your feet for a few days."

Dr. Johnson called me the next day and said the tests came back. He said, "You most likely have an infection called Osteomyelitis, but we need more tests to confirm that." I asked him what that was. Dr. Johnson said, "It's a disease of the bone." He said. "I'm going on vacation and I will set up the additional tests when I return home in three weeks. It's a slow process and there'll be plenty of time to put you in the hospital and treat it as soon as I get back from vacation. I hung up the phone. *Osteomyelitis, how could I have that?* Diabetics get that. My doctor had never told me I had diabetes.

I was getting very scared. I got this funny feeling that it's something really serious. There was only one thing that I could do. I turned it over to God. My first thought was that I was going to die, but quickly put that aside. I prayed *God I really need You right now. Please encircle me with Your love and let me feel Your warmth.* I wished the boys (Curt, fifteen and Todd, eleven) were home, but they were on a two-week vacation in Florida with their Dad and my grown son Chuck, twenty-four was working. He didn't live at home anymore.

Monday I worked, but the next day I was too sick to work. I called Dr. Johnson's office to find out if another doctor could see me. I was able to get in to see Dr. Gravlin on Tuesday and he referred me to Dr. Flaherty an orthopedic surgeon on Wednesday. On Friday Dr. Flaherty surgically removed the toenails from my two great toes at 10:00 a.m. at St. Francis Hospital.

I wasn't able to work the next few weeks. Thursday, August 16 was the start of a Cursillo weekend (a non-denominational spiritual

110

enrichment program.). Most of the Cursillos throughout the country are for Catholics only. Ours is the exception. I was a table leader on the team. It was held at St. Augustine Manor in Peoria. I went on the weekend, but had to leave the center to go see Dr. Flaherty on Friday. Then Friday night I was so sick that two people—Ron Thorne and Doyne Gaetz—took me to the Methodist Hospital emergency room (ER) to see Dr. Thomas, who also belonged to the Cursillo. Thomas prescribed a different antibiotic, Clindamycin. Thirty minutes after taking the first pill I had an allergic reaction and started itching all over. Thorne and Gaetz took me back to ER where I was given a third type of antibiotic.

Saturday I was so sick, I had to leave the conference center and go lay down. One of the team leaders came in my room to check on me. It was recommended that I go back to the hospital. This time we went to St. Francis and I was admitted.

There were over a hundred people there for the Cursillo weekend and every one of them was praying for me along with hundreds of others that heard about it during a church service. This was the first time in my life that I had experienced the magnitude of prayer firsthand. It was so powerful! I was very thankful for all of their support. I had so many people and ministers from various denominations coming to see me, it would be impossible to remember all of them.

I thought I was preparing myself, for nine weeks, to be on the Cursillo 245 team. Little did I know that God was preparing me for a much greater task. I remained for 9½ weeks with osteomyelitis. That was only a few days more than the preparation time for Cursillo. When I was too sick to pray, their prayers sustained me. I was surprised that I had so much peace and contentment during those difficult weeks. Their visits, cards, gifts and flowers also brightened those lonely days and nights. The memory will be with me for a long, long time. If I had not been on the team of 245 I'd never have gotten to know and love all of the wonderful team and candidates so well.

In the first week I was in the hospital, a friend from Cursillo, Faith Sanders, brought me a stack of books. I asked Faith, "Which one I should read first?" Without hesitation she said, *The Hiding Place*. Corrie ten Boom wrote the book along with John and Elizabeth Sherrill—presently writers for Guideposts magazine—whose writing I admire very much. That book was truly my salvation. Corrie and her sister Betsie's ordeal was not a mere 9½ weeks as mine was. They endured months and years of hiding from the Nazis and final imprisonment and torture by them in World War II. They had awful places to sleep, even with lice. When I needed a lift I would transport my mind to Corrie and Betsie's hiding place and pretend I was with them. This book left a profound impression on me. I'd have to classify Corrie's book with the *Diary of Anne Frank* and more recently *Schindler's List*.

After tests that confirmed I wasn't a diabetic, the only thing we could figure out was the fact that when Sears closed the decorator shop and put in the appliance department, where I had to stand up continually for eight or nine hours, I had to start wearing walking shoes. My pain was everywhere from fibromyalgia and my bad back. I had no idea that there was something separate going on with my toes—besides a not-too-significant fungus infection—that ended up being very significant in that it wasn't caught in time and led to osteomyelitis. I bought the new walking shoes when I was transferred to appliances and the top of the toe area of my shoes was hitting my two great toes and cutting off the circulation. It was difficult even walking out on the concrete parking lot to my car after standing that long on my feet. I would go home and collapse, too tired to even get me a snack or go to the bathroom.

Dr. Flaherty canceled my intravenous (IV) meds after being on antibiotics for only three weeks. A medical student walked in the next day and asked me what happened to my IV? I said, "Dr. Flaherty told me I didn't need it anymore."

She said, "But you have osteomyelitis." She rushed out of my room and got my chart. Tests showed that I definitely had osteomyelitis. She was able to get my IV started promptly. However, because of Dr. Flaherty's mistake, they had to start over with my treatment—I now had to endure six more weeks of IV's and hospitalization. At this point I felt it necessary to change doctors. Dr. Norman Mein was suggested to me by my niece, Amy Mahrt, who was a nurse.

Dr. Mein recommended that he amputate the part of my toe that was infected. I had a staph infection also from the toenail surgery. They alternated the antibiotics every two hours around the clock. Another doctor inserted a Broviac (permanent catheter) in my chest which was a godsend rather than getting needles stuck in my arms so frequently.

Dr. Richard O'Connor was my infectious disease doctor. He and Dr. Stephen Doughty were world renowned for their treatment of the twenty-eight botulism patients that ate at the Skewer Inn at Northwoods Mall in Peoria on October 18, 1983. One of those patients died. The botulism attacked their nervous system. The grilled onion on their patty melts was the culprit. Some people had the onions with their meal and they think the other people got botulism from cross-contamination with a utensil that had been used with the onions. What's ironical, Dr. O'Connor and his wife had also eaten dinner at the Skewer Inn that fateful day; although they didn't eat a patty melt. Dr. O'Connor was an absolutely wonderful, caring physician. One of the med students assigned to him was Carmen Scarimbola. I was so fortunate to have them take care of me while I was in St. Francis Hospital.

My sister Anne Rutledge (who was 14 months older than me) came to see me every day and I signed over my sick-pay checks to her so she could pay my bills for me. When Anne was unable to visit she'd send her husband Dwight to come to see me. They never missed a day.

Mom had never learned to drive a car, so my brother David brought her to see me. Mom (who was 79 years old at the time) looked so miserable when she came to visit. Part of that might have been because she was so worried about me. She also stayed with my two youngest sons Curt, 15 and Todd, 11 for a week. It was just too hard on her. She had a bad back most of her life and had colon cancer two years earlier.

My oldest son Chuck's girlfriend, at the time, stayed with Curt & Todd for a few days. When she came to visit me in the hospital she told me that the boys really didn't need her at all. I had taught them how to cook, wash clothes and clean house. The boys begged me to let them stay home. They didn't want to go to anyone else's house or miss school. None of my family lived in Pekin. I prayed about it and turned it over to God. I finally agreed to let them stay home by themselves, but they had to promise not to tell even their best friends that they were alone. I told them especially not to tell their dad, because he might try to take them away from me again. I talked to them every day and a friend from work, Cricket Burns used to check in on them also. Being without my sons for 9½ weeks was even worse than the disease itself. I missed them terribly. I was so proud of the way Curt and Todd handled this adversity.

When my former husband Larry found out I was in the hospital in Peoria, he picked the boys up every weekend—instead of the usual every other weekend—to stay with him. He also brought them to the hospital to see me and let them stay as long as they wanted. He'd wait downstairs in the lobby. That was truly a blessing. At least I was able to see the boys a few hours every weekend.

Dealing with all of the numerous roommates was quite an ordeal in itself. One man stayed with his wife all day every day. He was real short and wore high-heeled boots that made lots of noise when he walked. He couldn't sit still and walked around the room a lot. The couple was on public aid and his wife ordered double food for herself so her husband could eat all of his meals with her at the hospital—breakfast, lunch and supper. You might just as well say that I had both husband and wife as roommates. He stayed until bedtime usually. I had excruciating migraines quite often and any little sounds were annoying when I was that sick. I also threw up and had diarrhea with the migraines and her husband was usually in the way of me getting to the bathroom. It was right next to my roommate's bed. There was naturally no privacy at all.

My room was on the east side of the hospital and that allowed me to watch the sun come up every morning—at least when I didn't have a migraine. I didn't care if the nurses and doctors were blinded by the sun. It was truly the highlight of most of my days while I was there. I would open up the blinds at night so I could wake up to that beautiful sight. The sun was so spectacular shining on the towering twin spires of the Cathedral of St. Mary—where I made my first communion and attended my graduation ceremony from the Academy of Our Lady—that was taller than the houses surrounding it, as well as most of the trees. Farther in the distance was the Illinois River and the bluffs along the east side of the river were farther back yet.

While I was still in the hospital Mom was admitted a few days before her seventy-ninth birthday on the same floor of the hospital where I was, but in a different section. Her colon cancer returned. Now I understood why Mom seemed so miserable to me. My being sick probably added to her sickness. I was having a decent day on October seventh, the day of her birthday, so I walked down to Mom's hospital room. The hospital used to give everyone a bottle of sparkling soda water on their birthday (It looks like a bottle of champagne.) to celebrate with. Another sister Joanie brought in a cake. All of us seven girls were there. My only brother Dave was the only one missing. He might have been at work at the time the photo was taken.

On October ninth Mom had her second operation. I lay in my hospital bed getting another dose of an antibiotic. After her operation two of my sisters came down the hall to get me. I knew by the looks on their faces that the news wasn't good. When my IV med was finished all three of us walked down to meet the rest of my family in the waiting area by Mom's room. Her cancer was terminal this time. I didn't need that kind of news at that time. I walked back to my hospital room and cried my heart out. I was already going through the worst event in my life since my two divorces.

While I was in the hospital, a man from Cursillo, Rex Andrews came fairly often to see me. I didn't remember him, but I guess I served him food when he went through Cursillo. I volunteered for almost every Cursillo for many years, working in the kitchen, praying in the chapel or doing artwork. Rex and I became good friends after that. It helped me get through that stressful event in my life.

Due to my illness I was off work for eight months, which turned out to be a godsend, because it allowed me some extra time to spend with Mom.

Pastel painting Marjie Hickey Hull and the Rainbow

The Storm

Tuesday, April 23, 1985 was not one of my better days. I worked at Sears in Pekin, Illinois at the time selling carpeting. I was the only person in my department and that meant I was the one that measured, drew up the plans, placed the orders and took care of any problems that arose. This particular day everything seemed to go wrong that could. Worst of all was the fact that Mom was still in intensive care after having her third operation for colon cancer. My Mom emulated to me the steadfastness and strength to raise eight children alone with no support from my Dad—it was only through the grace of God that she got through it, but colon cancer was probably the toughest battle of her life.

I was getting ready to go out on a house call when I received a call from my sister Janet, saying that they had taken Mom out of intensive care. Mom was 80 years old then and I was very angry with God. Why was Dr. Roberts operating on her again? I thought *what's the use? Why not just let her die in peace?* It was painful to see her suffering so much. My anger had not subsided yet, even though I felt a sigh of relief that Mom was better.

Soon after the phone call I left for my appointment in the very small town of Green Valley. The sky was quite eerie looking. It was so dark that the sky appeared to blend in with the pavement. It took me about 30 minutes to get to Wanda Keim's house. She was a pleasant-looking woman, about 5'4" with dark brown hair and a wonderful disposition. I was thankful to end my day on a cheerful note. After I sold Wanda the carpeting I packed up my carpet samples and was heading out the door as Wanda held it open for me. She said in a surprised voice, "Oh! Look at the pretty rainbow!" I looked up at it and said, "Yes, that is pretty!" and I went about carrying the carpet samples to my 1980 Citation not truly grasping what I'd seen.

When I was leaving Green Valley, I turned left onto Toboggan Road—out in the country—and I got the surprise of my life. I felt like God picked up that rainbow that was in Green Valley and set it down right above and in front of my car. There were no farmhouses, trees or anything in between my car and the rainbow. There was nothing blocking my view. I could see every inch of it from one end to the other. Then I saw another rainbow standing separately in front of the main one with the colors reversed and softer hues. This second one didn't meet at the top. They were so close to the car that I felt like I could get out of the car and touch them. The rainbows were more beautiful than I could comprehend. They were awesome!

The next event that happened completely overwhelmed me. As I was driving along in awe of the beauty of it all, trying to catch the rainbows and soak up all I could before they dissipated, God had more for me showing me just how much control He really had in my life.

At the time I used to listen to WCIC—a Christian radio station out of Pekin—but my car radio had a loose wire and didn't work very well, especially in bad weather when it would drift off the station. When that happened, all I could hear was static. On this particular day while I was chasing the gorgeous rainbows I couldn't believe what I heard coming from my radio. It was the incomparable Judy Garland singing *Over the Rainbow*, written by E Y Harburg and composed by Harold Arlen. I thought, *Wow! Is this a dream?*

I could hardly believe that God allowed me to view such a spectacular sight and then to experience the gifted Judy Garland singing those glorious words! I was truly overwhelmed and tears welled up in my eyes, and then subsequently flowed freely down my bewildered face. The tears seemed to wash away all of the sadness and pain I felt deep down in my heart that day.

I felt God was saying to me, *be at peace, my daughter. My loving arms are wrapped around your Mother caring for her, giving her peace and preparing her to join Me soon in My house of many mansions. It's too big for you to handle.*

After I saw the rainbows I knew I didn't have to worry about Mom anymore. That last operation gave us another year with her that was very meaningful; for she told us many stories of her childhood that we had never heard before. She told us about Mary Elizabeth, the baby that died the day of her birth on February 6, 1926, and where she was buried. She was born before my brother Dave not after, like we always believed. Mom was pregnant before she married my Dad and none of us kids knew that. Her parents never found out either. Mom's last wish was to put a gravestone on Mary's grave. The cemetery couldn't find her grave, so we were unable to get a gravestone for Mary.

I treasure those moments I had with Mom after that last operation. When I saw her for the last time she looked more beautiful than I'd ever seen her, like a lovely sleeping angel dressed in her ivory-colored Qiana pajamas and coral-colored bathrobe both of which she made herself—so joyful and peaceful at last. I think God makes our loved ones look so wonderful so we can see the real beauty just before they're gone, like the trees with their gorgeous rainbow of fall colors just before they go to sleep for the winter.

The music of the rainbow I heard that spring day is synonymous with a Mother I hold dear that sang me cute perky songs—*I Love You a Bushel and a Peck, Daisy, Margie, I'm in Love with You Honey* to name a few— when I was a child and whose music and memory will always be tucked into the depths of my very being.

A Mother Is...

One who loves her children so tenderly
And in so doing raises them
To be loving too.

One who makes many sacrifices on their behalf
So they in turn would do that
For their own children.

One who teaches them to live a godly life by her examples
So they won't wonder
What is right and good.

One who's loving memory is—
And always will be—locked inside her children's hearts
For all eternity
Until they are reunited
In God's house of many mansions.

How wonderful that day will be
When all of heaven will rejoice
And sing praises
Befitting for one so special—Mother.

Marjie Hickey Hull's 100th Birthday Celebration

On October 7, 2005 it had been 19 years since Mom passed away. My brother, my sisters that lived in town, and I wanted to commemorate her 100th birthday. We decided on Fairchild's Her Majesty's English Tea Room in Dunlap, just outside Peoria. Mom drank tea all of her life, so the tearoom was an easy choice.

When we drove up to the restaurant, we were greeted by a quaint building nestled inside an English garden. A US flag hung boldly on the front sidewalk. The ground where the foliage was planted had unusual broken pottery pieces embedded in the ground. The walk leading up to the red door entrance was lined with beautiful foliage and—inlayed in the concrete sidewalk were stones with neat sayings on them. One of the stones said *Slow fairy crossing.* Another door to the tearoom said *Royalty is a state of mind.* How apropos! There was a scarecrow leaning up against the building.

We were entranced before we ever entered the tearoom. Once inside the tearoom we were not disappointed. Our waitress provided each of us sisters with a crown—representing a famous person—for each of us to wear. We could pick the one we wanted. Mine was Princess Di's. Dave was given a large red velvet crown with gold trim fit for a king. I thought, as I looked at Dave affectionately—*there he is sitting in all his royal splendor just like Mom wanted. I'll bet Mom is smiling down on us today.* We each got a three-tiered Lazy Susan with pastries to go along with our tea.

The tearoom was simply gorgeous with all kinds of unusual gifts you could purchase. There were things everywhere; teapots, tiaras, baskets, clothes—and among all of the treasures was a real, full-sized, black Austin automobile inside the restaurant. I could hardly wait to do the scrapbook pages for that day. It'll really be fun. We'll have to go back and do it again when my sisters Susie and Pat come back to Peoria.

Second Chances

On September 17, 2006 *Parade Magazine* (that comes with our Sunday Peoria Journal Star (PJS) newspaper) had a wonderful article written by Mitch Albom, author of *For One More Day.* *"If you had one more day with someone who's gone…"* about what you would do with a loved that died if you had one more day to be with them, and asked the public to respond to that question at *www.parade.com*. Albom, was coming to Peoria on October 12 to promote his new book along with promoting a fundraiser for a local organization—Family House—that offers low income out-of-town people, a place to stay, when a family member is hospitalized or in a nursing home.

The story stirred up so much interest in Peoria that, on September 24th, PJS asked the local readers to respond to the question, "Which loved ones that have passed away would you most like to see just one more time and what would you do when you were with them?" I thought, *I'll send them the story about Mom and the rainbow.* I quickly wrote a letter and emailed it to the PJS. It wasn't published in the newspaper, but it was on their website.

Tea for Two

The following story written by Terry Hickey Abercrombie was on the Peoria Journal Star website in October 2006—used with permission of PJS:

"I would love to spend one more day with Mom on October 7. That would be her 101st birthday. Mom raised us eight kids by herself. What a saint she was. She died in 1986. Mom didn't drink coffee or soda pop, just tea wherever she went. Last year on her 100th birthday our sister Anne from Florida was in town so Dave, Joanie, Janet and I went with Anne (Pat and Susie lived out of town) to a teahouse in Dunlap—Fairchild's Her Majesty's English Tea Room—and celebrated Mom's hundredth birthday. We had a wonderful day. Mom had only one boy and seven girls and my brother was the oldest. I always told people that we all treated Dave like royalty (per Mom's request), because Dave helped Mom financially to raise us girls.

"I wrote a story about Mom in 1985 while she was still alive. I was really upset with God that He was putting her through so much pain and also with her doctor for putting her through another operation (her third one). She had colon cancer.

"I would love to get my sister Susie from California, Anne from Florida, Pat from O'Fallon, Illinois and all of us in town, Dave, Janet, Joanie and me and go back to the Teahouse to have the best celebration ever. Of course Mom would have to come and my sister Shirlee that passed away on February 17, 1990. I'm going to print out my little story with maybe a picture from the teahouse and give to everyone. I had also written a poem about Mom. My sister Joanie tried to read it to Mom one day while I was visiting her, but Mom started crying real hard and Joanie had to stop. Mom was very sensitive and didn't want to talk about dying. She had always gotten her feelings hurt easily so I was afraid to read the story to her either. I did tell her about the rainbow I saw and the music, but didn't discuss how I felt about her operation or anything. She never knew I wrote the story about her.

"I received all of Mom's sewing supplies after her death. I make handmade greeting cards with her beautiful lace and trimmings on the cards. I would make Mom a gorgeous birthday card. I think she would be surprised, but happy to see what I'm doing with the trimmings. They really look nice on the greeting cards—Terry Hickey Abercrombie"

Responses to The Storm Story

Amy Rutledge Dunaway RN, my niece from Peoria, Illinois wrote:

"The Little Things

"I'm not much of a detail oriented person. My memories are not filled with details of gatherings – who was there or even what happened unless it was a momentous or tragic occasion. I've always looked at, and stored to memory, the big picture.

"As I look back on my memories of Grandma, all I see is gentleness and love. In looking at the big picture, I knew Grandma loved me. She loved me in little ways. She greeted me by name each and every time we visited. I was never glossed over in the crowd of grandchildren that gathered frequently at her home. She called me by name and offered some little tidbit that let me know she was keeping up with my life.

"As I grew up, we had more grown-up kinds of conversations with a mutuality bound by love of grandmother and granddaughter. We talked mostly about the little things – precious little things. I observed, listened and incorporated what was good and lovely about her.

"I only have a picture to recall the details of her face and gentle smile. A smile as lovely as her little garden where life stopped for sips of mint iced tea. A place where I was enveloped by love, could relax and enjoy our time together. The soft scent of roses filled the air as conversation revolved around little things.

"I'll always associate Grandma with Christmas and the gathering of family. A special time filled with love, stories and laughter. We know a few are missing and missed but the love continues on with a sense of their presence no matter where we are.

"As Grandma aged and fought a courageous battle with cancer, I was honored and blessed to hold her hand during extremely painful procedures. Her hands were very soft and warm and the tears she cried fell on our hands as she endured pain that few will know. Tears I treasure to this day.

"As she became weaker and knew her time was coming, I held her hand as she slipped into a state marked by mumbling and what others saw as confusion. I listened carefully as she talked to God, working out her mistakes with her Lord and Savior. She didn't mind my presence so I sat at her bedside holding her soft, warm hand in the sterile environment that is life in the hospital basking in the love of Grandma – and her love for God as she prayed and asked forgiveness for her sins.

"Certainly those were sad times as we watched this gentle, lovely soul prepare to leave us. It was such a comfort to know she was prepared and ready.

"It is in these little things that the big picture tells its story. The story of love and the gentleness of her soul – and everything a grandma should be. Grandma showed me the meaning of this life. It is all about love in the little things and little ways in which we love one another so the big picture can tell the story.

"She has gone ahead but we know her soul is safe – may she rest in peace and rise in glory..."

Chris Spong Phillips, my niece from Santa Cruz, California wrote:

"This is so wonderful. It amazes me how much Grandma Margie touched all of us. When I sent off that latest "getting to know me" type email, my sister Theresa said to the question "who or what do you miss the most", she missed Grandma the most! I said my health. As soon as I saw what she wrote, I thought about how much I miss her and how I prayed for God to touch her and worried about her being in heaven with us. When she stayed with us and was sick, Mom was out of town and she had had a problem at Shirlee's so she came to stay with us. I will never forget that time. I was a nervous wreck. I wanted to fix things for her to make her more comfortable, clean my house, fix food she liked, talk to her and enjoy her, and I felt so worthless. I was so happy to see her but so sad and nervous at the same time. I wish I could change the nervousness into peace so I could have enjoyed her more. She was too sick to eat much. She was in a lot of pain and wanted to sleep a lot. This is when her cancer came back. She was visiting our family in California. We gave her Jeanne's room and hoped she'd be comfortable in there. I loved her so much but was nervous to be around her. It had been too many years since I had seen her and talked to her.

"I am so glad you have such wonderful memories! It warms my heart to hear how God told you to not worry about her. He knows what we need to calm our spirits and show us His wonderful miracles.

"Thanks for sharing with us! I love to read your stories! Love, Chris"

Dave Hickey (deceased), my Brother (Father) said:

> "When Mom had her three operations, she had the same nurse prepping her for surgery each time. That was unusual at such a large hospital. The day Mom died, August 27, 1986, that same nurse came to see her and had tears in her eyes.

> "When you (Terry) took me to the same hospital when I had prostate cancer and they operated on me, that same nurse took care of me and when I went for a test at OSF Center for Health, she was there also."

Mom was still looking after Dave from above.

Chuck Perry, my oldest son from Highlands Ranch Colorado:

> "Hi mom, Very cool that this got printed. My best memory is the day I stayed all night with Grandma and Uncle Dave when I was around five years old and Grandma asked me what I wanted for breakfast. It was Saturday and Uncle Dave was making a pot of chili (which he does every Saturday morning). I told her I wanted ice cream."

> "Grandma said, 'Chuckie, you know your Mom wouldn't want you to have ice cream for breakfast.'"

> "I said, 'Well, Uncle Dave has unusual breakfasts.' Grandma told that story to everyone."

Denise Seader Perry, my daughter-in-law from Highlands Ranch, Colorado:

> "Hey Terry – your articles were great. What a great story you got published. Hope you are doing well. Love Denise"

Curt Abercrombie, my second son from Florence, Kentucky:

> "When I was about nine years old I was over at Grandma's house reading a comic book and a St. Louis

Cardinal sticker fell out of the book. I got so excited that it was in a comic book. I didn't think about it for a long time. Once I was grown up and recalled that, I think Grandma must have slipped the sticker in the book when I wasn't looking.

"In 1984 I was with my Mom, and my brother Todd at Grandma's getting our pictures taken with Uncle Dave and Grandma Marjie. A professional photographer was taking outdoor pictures of us. I loved that. This was just before her cancer reoccurred and just before we found out it was terminal."

Todd Abercrombie, my youngest son from Peoria, Illinois:

"That was a nice story about Grandma. I don't know if I ever made the connection between your love of rainbows and the song. It was very moving. Love Todd"

Anne Hickey Rutledge, my sister from Port St. Lucie, Florida:

"I remember walking with Mom in a flower garden. Mom would keep stopping to admire each one. She loved all flowers.

"Mom dressed up like a fashion model and looked like she just stepped out of a fashion magazine. She looked beautiful in hats and everyone noticed her when we went anywhere. Once Mom, my brother Dave and I were at a Bob Evans restaurant when another patron was paying her bill and she walked back to our table and told Mom how beautiful she looked.

"Another time Mom and I were traveling to visit Mumsie (Grandma Leone Killey). I was making a U-turn and a policeman pulled me over. Mom said, "I'm sorry we were talking and went past the turn-off. It's entirely my fault." The policeman let us go without writing up a ticket. Mom could charm anyone."

Kay Rutledge, my niece from Arizona:

"Dear Aunt Terry, Thank you so much for sharing these stories with me. They are beautiful and I must confess I shed a few tears while reading them. I miss Grandma so much . . . . I think of her all the time. When I look at the stars at night . . . . I imagine she is sitting on the brightest one . . . . watching over us all. She was so much to me in so many ways . . . . one of the few people who really understood me. She gave me great advice . . . . that I still follow to this day. She was bigger than life . . . . we are so blessed to have had her in our lives, as we are blessed to have you to write such wonderful memories, and to create beautiful cards and poems, I see so much of Grandma in her children . . . . I'll never forget sitting with her on her patio on a beautiful May day . . . . enjoying the flowers and a hummingbird or two. She shared with me that she looked at her children as her proudest accomplishment . . . . she called you all her flower garden. She was proud of how her garden had grown and flourished.

"Thanks for sending me the articles . . . . "I hope to see you soon. Take care and write when you can. Love, Kay"

Kathy Dean Davis, my niece from Creve Coeur, Illinois:

"This is a neat story. I really appreciate you sending it to me to read. I love getting things like this. Thank you. Love Kathy"

Clowning Around

In 1988 I decided to make a couple of clown suits to use when I was in the *Gut Bucket Band* on many Cursillo weekends. I was hoping that no one would recognize me in my clown suit, but they knew who I was right away. (We dressed in funny clothes, but we sang beautiful songs like *Amazing Grace* and other songs familiar to most people, along with some comical songs, guitar and banjo players, drum players and someone would tell a few jokes. It was always different, depending on who showed up on a particular night). We would go in on Saturday evening. Most of the people in the band had wonderful voices and played instruments really well. I loved to sing with them, but I didn't have a good voice so I sang quietly.

I would also go visit a few people on their birthdays in my clown suit. My sister Anne and her best friend Mary Jo Voris Williams still get together for birthdays with their spread from high school. On one of Anne's birthdays (November 22) they went to Jumer's Castle Lodge restaurant for dinner. I decided to take Anne balloons in my clown suit and surprise her. I took my regular clothes with me so I could change into regular clothes to exit the restaurant. Mary Jo invited me to stay and paid for my dinner. I always enjoyed being around Anne's friends and especially Mary Jo.

There weren't many people that knew that I did clowning. I really enjoyed it, but after I had a portion of my left great toe amputated I quit doing it. I fell quite a few times after that. My costume had a big hoop in it to make me look fatter, but making it impossible to see where I was walking. I could have just made a different kind of clown suit, but I never did.

The Heart of a Clown

This morning I put on my clown suit.
Spent hours applying my makeup.
It's so much fun being a clown.
When I'm a clown, it's almost like I'm somebody else.
Sometimes it's easier than being myself.

You see, when I'm just me, I have all kinds of tribulations.
I might have just lost a loved one.
My children might have been bad today.
I don't have money to make my car payment or
There's a leak in the roof and so on.

Today I'm Rainbow the clown
I'm able to transform myself
From an ordinary person to an unusual clown
A clown that has the ability
To make children of all ages laugh and sing.

If you knew the real hurts that are inside me
I couldn't be a very effective clown
So I must put on a façade
To camouflage the real me.

I have a mission
One that comes from God.
Through Him and only through Him
Do I have the capability of being a clown.

It's kind of nice to be somebody else for awhile
When I look into your laughing eyes
As I do some of my funny tricks
I'm overcome with joy.

Don't you look back into my eyes;
For I wear lots of makeup so you can't see them.
The eyes are the windows of the soul
And you'd surely see the deep sadness.

But sometimes I want to be me
So I can cry out to you.
That's when I especially need the help of the Lord
To overcome that.

If you happen to see my sad eyes
In one of my weak moments
Just pretend you didn't,
But pray for me instead
For I have needs and wants just like you
Sometimes my heart is very sad.

No matter what I look like on the outside
Whether I'm in my clown suit or not
The inside of me is still the same
So please be my friend;
For I have a loving, compassionate heart
The heart of a clown
And it belongs to Jesus.

Tattered Pockets—Hidden Hopes

As I sat on the sofa in my living room, ripping pockets and belt loops off my youngest son Todd's old worn-out, denim blue jeans, I wondered if that was such a good idea after all. Denim fabric is very heavy and the factories usually use heavy-duty thread and double seams throughout. I turned on the television to break the monotony. I recalled the reason I was doing that—the beautiful vest that Shirley Adams from the *Sewing Connection* television show so cleverly fashioned from old jeans. When I saw that I thought maybe I could come up with something original for the old jeans too. I love a challenge and I'd been designing my own clothes and decorations for my home for most of my life. I rationalized that it would be worth it when I see my finished designs.

Old blue jeans! It's ironic how one person might not give it a second thought to trashing the jeans, while some of us could see possibilities. If you saw the numerous boxes of fabric I already had, you might wonder why I would bother with this old fabric with all the new fabric I had to sew with. Old clothes—especially blue jeans—have a character all their own and I'm always looking for something unusual to challenge my resourcefulness.

Then my mind wanders off to Saturday, February 3, 1990 the day before my fiftieth birthday. That's the day Todd and I had to be out of our townhouse in Pekin. I lost my last job in October 1989 due to carpal tunnel. I called Carol Shyers—the mother of Todd's best friend Kevin Young—to see if Todd could stay with their family for a few days.

"Oh, that would be fine," said Carol. "Steve (her husband) and I think the world of him. Where will you stay?"

I said, "I don't have a place yet." My first concern was for Todd.

She said, "We have an extra bedroom if you'd like to stay here too. Todd can sleep with Kevin on his large waterbed."

I didn't know them very well, but I loved Kevin like my own son. I figured his parents must be special people to raise a son like him. I found that my assumption was correct. The Shyers were absolutely wonderful to Todd and me.

Two weeks later on February 17, 1990 my oldest sister Shirlee passed away unexpectedly. She was in the hospital in Sacramento, California (where she had moved 30 years ago) with possible Legionnaires' disease. She died very early the very morning she was to be released to go home.

Without a job, there was no way I could go to Shirlee's funeral. I was still living with Carol and Steve Shyers in Pekin then. I went to the post office the morning of her funeral. As I tried to exit the parking lot I had to wait for a funeral procession to pass by. I pulled out as soon as it was safe. I felt warm all over as I followed the procession—like I was with Shirlee's procession in California—and tears started flowing down my face. My sister Anne called after the funeral was over. I asked her what time the funeral took place. I was not really shocked to find out that it was going on while I was following that procession. I felt my sister's spirit before I found out when the funeral actually took place. *Thank You Lord.* I was elated that God allowed me to participate at Shirlee's funeral in spirit even though—in reality—I was 3,000 miles away. I was also happy that they played her favorite song *Avé Maria* at the funeral.

About a week after Shirlee's funeral my sister Anne called again and said, "Shirlee left her life insurance and house to us seven siblings." We were all shocked at that. None of us had any idea. She changed her will after Mom died in 1986—leaving out her four children. We didn't feel right about taking all of the money and we gave her kids and only grandchild a portion.

Todd and I stayed with the Shyers family for six weeks then moved in with my brother Dave in Peoria. I was surprised that I wasn't able to find a house that I could afford in Peoria either. It was very expensive storing my furniture for eleven months. I had two storage units.

The following September while I was still at my brother's house, I received a call from Terry McLaughlin, the wife of Tom, one of my high school friends. They belonged to Holy Family Catholic Church where I attended.

Terry said, "I just finished schooling to become a Realtor. If you haven't found a house yet, I wonder if you'd like me to help you find a place to rent."

"I would love your help, but I might be able to buy a house. Do you think there are any houses available in the area contract for deed?

My oldest sister died and left me some money." With no full time job I figured it would be difficult to buy a house the conventional way.

"I'll see if I can find out for you," Terry said.

There was only one house in Peoria for sale contract for deed. The owners had just taken the house off the market because the three-month listing had expired with the realty company. Terry called the owners to see if it was still for sale. It was. I wasn't too optimistic, because it was in one of the older sections of the city on the west side where some of the homes were pretty run down. I was willing to go look at it. Terry and I went to view the house the very next day. I had a part-time job at St. Francis Hospital through Kelly Temporary Services by now, but I didn't have much extra cash to spare. It would take every penny I had for the down payment and moving expenses.

As we pulled up to the house at 2101 N North Street the exterior looked good with pale yellow aluminum siding, a separate garage and one large oak tree in the front yard and another in the back. We went up the front steps to the large porch that stretched across the whole front of the house. I noticed two ceiling hooks that probably once held a porch swing. My mind drifts off for a minute to when I was a young girl. *Someone we visited had a swing on their front porch. When I would swing on it, something magical would happen. I would dream of better times with a big house and a bedroom—or at least a separate bed—for each one of us eight kids. I dreamed of pretty new clothes instead of hand-me-downs. I dreamed that my Dad was with us to watch us grow up. All too soon my dreams would end and we'd have to go home to our four-room house in the south end of Peoria.*

Many years have passed since that dream took place. As we walked in the front door I felt a calm I could not explain. I thought *could this be the house?* We stepped onto new beige sculptured carpeting that extended into the dining room. Straight ahead from the front door was a was a fantastic brick fireplace with a mantel of solid oak—just like the wood trimming on the vast amount of windows and door ways. *My crèche would look great on the mantel at Christmas.* The ceilings were eight feet high. The wallpaper had a pale gold background with delicate orange and brown flowers. There were windows everywhere. The living room and dining room each had one wall with a set of three leaded glass windows set up high on the walls. The dining room had a crystal chandelier that gave a prism effect with the sunlight dancing around the room through the leaded glass windows.

The kitchen had new vinyl floorcovering, a new sink and new cabinets. The basement was completely finished. It had a new shower and bathroom fixtures. The same carpeting as the downstairs continued up the imposing staircase and into the hall of the upstairs where we found three bedrooms and another full bath.

As we continued through the rest of the house, I kept thinking something would show up to discourage me from wanting the house, but there was nothing. Everything was tastefully and well done throughout the home. There would be plenty of room for my sewing/art room and even an extra bedroom for my middle son, Curt who was at Western Illinois University, studying for a business administration degree. *God, is this home going to be mine?* It seemed like this house was designed specifically for me and my furniture. There was so much character and charm in this home. By now I didn't care that the home was not in a better part of town.

I went back to my brother's house and slept on it. I was unable to think of anything but that house. I knew I didn't have enough money right then for the down payment. I prayed, *God, if it's your will, help me find a way to buy that house.* I called Terry the next day after much contemplation and praying and said, "I'd like to put in a bid on the house." The rest of my sister Shirlee's inheritance, wouldn't be released until February or March.

"Okay, that's great. What will be your proposal?"

"I'll put down $1,000 now in earnest money," I said, "I'll pay rent for two or three months until the rest of my money arrives and will pay the balance of the down payment at that time. One more thing—I want to move in before Christmas."

Terry said, "I've never heard of anyone being allowed to move into a home before they've made the full down payment. I don't think they'll let you do that."

"That's how I want to do it," I said, "If the Lord wants me to have that house, they'll agree to my proposal. If God doesn't want me to have it, they'll say no."

The day after Thanksgiving I heard a song, *I'll Be Home for Christmas.* I love that song. I've always been a sentimentalist. I pictured me having that home on North Street by Christmas. I kept praying to God about it—knowing that He was the only One that could really make it happen.

135

Two days later I received a call from Terry saying that Doc and Helen Harwood—the owners of the house—agreed to my proposal. I was elated. We were able to move in on December 10, 1990. A few days later Terry came over with a thank you gift, a hand-painted crèche that I put on the oak mantel right away. It was hand painted and much nicer than the one I already had. What a special Christmas that was. My oldest son, Chuck Perry from Denver, was able to join us for the holidays.

We have watched *The Miracle on 34th Street* with James Stewart and Donna Reed every holiday season and that movie took on a whole new meaning for me. Christmas 1990 was a Christmas I'll never forget; for we had our own *Miracle* on North Street. In reflecting back on the happenings of that year, God had a purpose for everything I went through. Maybe God just wanted me to write this story to inspire others not to give up, when the going gets tough. It was all part of His plan for me—although I paid a pretty price for it. Losing my sister Shirlee was the hardest part. I have peace and joy knowing that she's in a better place now with my Mom and Dad. Todd and I were without a home for eleven months, but the wait was well worth it. It made us appreciate the house all the more.

Getting back to the pockets and belt loops I was ripping off of Todd's old jeans—the worthiness of someone or something is a matter of perception. One person might see impossibility while others see possibility. God blessed me with a creative mind, and I frequently find something useful to make out of what the average person might see, as not good for anything. My sons used to joke about my saving things to recycle before that was the *in* thing to do. Now it's not a joke. I made many things for my kitchen from those old blue jeans. I made placemats, potholders, towels, and even covered a Campbell's soup can with the denim and used it to hold napkins, pencils, etc. I sold the designs and the directions for making them to a national magazine.

I compare my life now as being recycled like the denim jean pockets. I used to do my own thing rather than doing what a child of God should do. God in His great wisdom saw possibilities for my tattered and torn life—like the tattered pockets. Recycling me is an ongoing process. I hope that there's still a lot of good left in me in God's eyes to make recycling me beneficial for many years to come. The worthiness of my life is a matter of perception in God's eyes and

I'm so utterly thankful that He deals in tattered lives—where He sees the hidden hopes of my torn life and a future with Him in heaven—in His house of many mansions.

In the Holy Name of Jesus

Just lend a helping hand or two
To all those that you meet.
Show them how much you care for them
In Jesus's name so sweet.

If someone wants to slap your face,
Show them the other side.
Offer it up to Jesus Christ;
For Jesus meek and mild.

For God will bless you tenderly
On that last judgment day.
He'll say, "Because you listened well,
In heaven you may stay."

The sadness we endure right now
Should be in Jesus's name.
And 'cause His dying on that cross
For us—is why He came.

Oh bless His Holy Name!
Oh bless His Holy Name!

The World Trade Center and the Pentagon—9/11

I was getting ready to go to my art class at Illinois Central College when I watched in disbelief as the World Trade Center burned on September 11, 2001. I never dreamed that such a horrible thing could happen in the U.S. As I walked out to my car after my art class, everyone was gathered around their cars listening to their radios. It reminded me of the scenes I've seen about the bombing of Pearl Harbor by the Japanese, when families were crowded around their console radios, listening to the events that were taking place that day.

This year is the tenth anniversary of the World Trade Center disaster. In the December 2001 issue of *Guideposts* magazine, I read a story written by John DeVito along with Elizabeth Sherrill called, *The Faces of Hope,* about his experience on the day of the World Trade Center disaster. DeVito was chief operating officer at May Davis on the eighty-seventh floor of Tower One, an investment company that helps raise money for small businesses to get started. It was such an inspiring and powerful story that I felt compelled to write a poem about it called:

Somebody's Eyes

A man rushed down the steps that day
He did not have much time to pray
He had a water jug in hand
His taking it was just unplanned.

His sight was dimmed from smoke-filled halls
From injured people, heard their calls
He met a fireman very hot,
"This water will cool you down a lot."

The fireman paused; removed his hat
But there was just no time to chat

The fireman said he'd need no water;
For he was on his way up yonder.

The fireman's eyes were all aglow
He'd be in heav'n soon, you know.
He donned his hat and said, "Good day!"
Then grabbed some people on his way.

How could it be? Was this John's cue
In this great life to bid adieu?
And he was stunned just for a flash
Where heav'n and hell had surely clashed.

This man, who seemed to recognize
The fireman with the warm blue eyes
Continued down the endless stairs
Entertained angels unawares.

The man gave water, then hurried about
Could he do more was his cloud of doubt?
He didn't do so very much
Just some water—a human touch.

Viewing the image of those eyes,
Just one more chance that John surmised,
At life, so he should trod on out
Sharing his water 'round about.

What was really such a surprise
The Jesus he saw in somebody's eyes
Was just a reflection of his own face
And truly from God's holy grace.

SAYING GOODBYE

Heavenly Dance

Rememb'ring not so long ago
At Spalding CYC,
When I first laid my eyes on you
And watched you dance with glee.

I waited oh so anxiously
—It seemed to take so long—
For you to ask me for a dance
To Elvis Presley's song.

It didn't matter then how short
You were in actual height.
Your personality was tops
Your feet were oh so light.

You couldn't dance much as of late
But mem'ries of back then
Are fresh now as you dance your way
Right on up to heaven.

Missing You Daughter

Rememb'ring when you were so small
Seems just like yesterday
When I would glimpse your sparkling eyes,
And watch you hard at play.

As time passed by I watched each phase
Of life unfold for you
Ponytails, puppies, kitty cats,
Just to name a few.

Finally you were all grown up
With children of your own.
Then it was time to say goodbye
—too soon—so all alone.

I visualize my daughter sweet
Another you love dear.
Just know that when I join you there
I'll hold you oh so near.

Peanut

God sent a special angel down
To touch and bless the fold
A tiny babe much smaller than
His great big heart of gold.

This little guy was very strong
And fought with all his might
To stay here with his family
Though heav'n his final plight.

I think he earned his halo here
In his short time on earth
The impact of his life on all
Did surely win a berth.

So when you're out and feel the breeze
Blow soft against your face
'Tis Peanut throwing you a kiss.
Seize the moment—embrace.

Beyond the Morrow

Some people come into our lives and leave a lasting impression. You are one of those people. You are very special to me and I find it difficult to tell you goodbye, because that sounds so final and I don't want our relationship to end.

You have exemplified what a true Christian should be in the kind things you say and do. There are not many people in my life that have left such an impression on me. I just want you to know that wherever you go just remember one thing—that I'll be thinking of you often; especially when I see a butterfly. For butterflies remind me of renewal and you have certainly renewed my faith in God. When I first met you I was like a caterpillar and you taught me how to spin a cocoon and become a beautiful butterfly in God's eyes. No words can adequately express how much that means to me.

No one in my life has ever affected my relationship with God as much as you have. You brought out the best in me and I thank you for that.

In the meantime, I wish you the best because you deserve it. May God bless you and be with you in all your endeavors. I will never forget you.

Once in a Blue Moon

My landlady stopped by my house today to tell me she was putting the house up for sale and I'd have to move. I was devastated. It was so hard to find housing for my 16-year old son, Todd, and me that I could afford in Pekin. I was dating a wonderful Christian man. I called him and told him the news and asked him if he could meet me at Steak N Shake for coffee.

After we had coffee and a snack, he took me for a ride out in the country. It was May 31, 1988. The Peoria CBS TV affiliate weatherman, Chuck Collins, said there would be a blue moon that night. My friend wanted me to see it. I was so surprised that the moon was copper, not blue. *Thank You, God! It was such a special blessing to be lifted from despair on such a dismal day. I never doubt your presence, Lord. It was so evident in that glorious copper moon, all aglow and shimmering in the night sky on my friend's face—and especially in his eyes.*

The Copper Glow of Eventide

The birds were quiet. The toads were still.
The sun was down. The hoot owls trilled.
The leaves were rustling in the night so dim
Flying squirrels swished from limb to limb.

The crickets chirped as they went to feed.
The full moon rose so slowly indeed.
The night was young with the stars in tow.
The moon was copper and all aglow.

I'll never forget his caring style
When we were together for a while
And his love for God that night in June
When we viewed that copper-colored moon.

A Brother Farewell

My brother, Dave Hickey, died yesterday, September 25, 2011. He had had two earlier bouts with prostate cancer, melanoma and congestive heart failure. He was in an auto accident right before Father's Day this year. He didn't have any physical injuries, but I could see a big difference in him otherwise. When he went to the doctor, the doctor discovered that he had a tumor in his liver. The doctor said his heart was worse and he only had six to twelve months to live. Dave decided not to take chemo, because the doctor said his heart would give out before his liver and the chemo wouldn't cure his liver anyway.

Dave was the oldest of eight children in our family and the only boy (I am the youngest). When he was about twelve, he took a bicycle apart and made himself a go-cart. I have a picture of Dave riding the go-cart. Dad wasn't too pleased when he found out, but that was the start of his technical talents that grew on to much bigger things.

When he was fourteen he quit school and went to work to help Mom support us. He had dyslexia. I don't think people knew what that was back when he was in school. He got held back one year and ended up in our sister Shirlee's class. She was one year younger than him. That was just devastating for him, because she was so brilliant in everything scholastically. Dave was outstanding in everything but reading, even though his peers might not have noticed.

He loved to take just about anything apart—toasters, radios or anything he could get his hands on. When he grew up he also was a genius at fixing cars—as well as his unbelievable amount of patience in everything he did.

Dave joined the Navy when he was seventeen, ending up in Okinawa as World War II was winding down. A little over a year later, one year after he joined the Navy, the money he sent home wasn't enough to take care of all of us. Dave had listed all of us —Mom and us seven girls—as dependents. She sent a letter to the Navy requesting an honorable discharge for him. The Navy let him out, although Dave wanted to stay in. He had already formed a strong bond with the guys in his unit. He never complained about it and went back home where he was badly needed. He felt it was his duty to help Mom.

When he was older he bought a set of encyclopedias and loved to read them. He also could work very difficult crossword puzzles. He loved to watch true stories on television about science or anything educational. He never quit learning.

We moved to 106 Widenham Street in the south end of Peoria in 1948. He started ordering Heath Kits through the mail and made our first television set, radios, or just about anything electrical. He worked for Peoria Cartage (trucking) Company for many years on the docks unloading heavy cargo from the trucks. When televisions first came out, he also worked for United Radio and TV installing TV antennas on roofs. Back then everyone knew who had televisions, by the high antennas that protruded from the rooftops. He gave almost all of his checks to Mom and would keep a little money to run around on. I can remember walking down to Walt Barden's tavern—where Dave always went on Fridays to cash his checks—to get money for Mom, because she needed it right away.

He lived with Mom all of his life except for his stint in the Navy and was a great comfort for Mom until her death in 1986. Dave passed away on my oldest sister Shirlee's birthday. She passed away February 17, 1990. I'm sure they had a great celebration in heaven when Dave arrived. The morning just before his death, one of the nurses asked Dave what was his favorite meal that Mom used to make? My sister Joanie was with him when he died and told the nurse that he loved her pork loin roasts with mashed potatoes and gravy. The nurse told Dave that Mom was already preparing the dinner for him in preparation for his arrival in heaven. The fish should be biting also as he resumes his favorite pastime—while he was on earth—after the feast. He was quite the fisherman.

So Long My Friend

Dixie (my friend for twenty-five years from Caterpillar) was a wonderful friend. She was the assistant to my boss, Burl Shelor (deceased). She never acted like she was above me by the caring way she handled every situation. She knew how to get respect from all of us keypunch operators anyway. There were stories going around about me. Most were untrue. Dixie did not judge me—she was my friend anyway. She treated me like I was somebody special. I took her to some of our retirement parties or when something special was going on that was work related. She never learned how to drive, so I was conscious of that and offered to pick her up. I loved being around her, even though I didn't really know she was a Christian at the time.

When Dixie retired, she and her husband Bill—who retired as a sergeant with the Peoria Police Department—lived in Canada part of the year. She came home when her sister died in 1990 and I saw her at the funeral. We planned to go out to eat on a Saturday morning before she went back to Canada. Bill called me the night before. He said, "Dixie is gone." I said, "So when will she be back?" I still wanted to go to breakfast with her sometime and I couldn't comprehend what he was really telling me. He said, "No, she had a heart attack while taking a shower and died instantly." It was so sad to lose such a good friend I'd had for so long. I will never forget Dixie and her acceptance of me as her friend—even though I wasn't a Christian. She is the reason I became one.

BIRTHDAYS

Nick's Birthday Wish

Your birthday is an awesome time
To reminisce with you
The day we made those valentines—
Cheyenne and Ethan too.

You really touched my heart that day
With one you made for me
My fav'rite blue with lots of hearts
Just filled my heart with glee.

The candy was a real nice touch
The hugs you gave–just right.
Our trip to Allenstown was great
The Stanley quite a sight.

I watched you doing Ju Jitsu.
I visited your school.
I photographed you goofing off.
You surely were real cool.

But what I recall most in you
Is your sweet loving heart.
It's bigger than the whole of you
Of which I do impart.

So when I miss you I just reach
Into my heart and feel
That you are with me anyway
And that is such a deal.

Birthday Wishes for a Friend

When I think about the years that have passed
And all the happenings thereof,
I marvel at the workings of God in our lives.
Only He knows what's in store
For the coming year.

One thing I know for sure is that it'll be a year
For new beginnings and renewal of things past.
These are promises we can count on;
For the Lord in His great wisdom
Has many new avenues for us to examine.

What do I wish most for your birthday?
That you have a wonderful day
And that the year to come
Is filled with all you hoped for
And things you might never have imagined.

Friends

Good friends are sometimes hard to find
Along with ones who're fun and kind.
So on your special day I wish
A Happy Birthday full of bliss!

Beer Wishes

Birthdays seem to come so often
It's just another year.
Let's quit counting how old we are
Just have an ice-cold beer.

A beer to celebrate the day
A beer wish for good health.
A beer because you are still here
The last one's for some wealth.

If you can't drink four beers
Have a great day anyway!

Celebrate

Birthdays seem to come and go
So swiftly as of late.
Why does time fly by so fast?
I can't anticipate.

All I know is yours is here
So you must bid adieu—though
Last year's dreams are this year's hopes
And God has plans for you.

Don't you fret about this day
That signifies your fate.
Who recalls how young you are?
Not me. So celebrate!

Happy Anyway Sister

A birthday here, a birthday there
Time to add another
Oh me, oh my, what can we do?
Should we really bother?

Too many candles for the cake
Too many years to count
But if we can't see the wrinkles come
We too can't see them mount.

So after donning your makeup
Turn down the lights real low
If your hair doesn't look real good
Don a hat with a bow.

Wrinkles are shadowed with a hat
Your face will softly glow
Follow these orders to the "T"
Then listen to and fro.

People will notice the hat first thing
Then see your smiling face
They'll say, *"Oh my, you look so young!"*
Take compliments with grace.

Have a wonderful birthday!
(PS: The advice is for when you get much older).

For a Son on Turning Fifty

A birthday here, a birthday there,
Time to add another.
Oh me! Oh my! What can we do?
Should we really bother?

Too many candles for the cake.
Too many years to count.
But if we can't see the wrinkles come,
We too can't see them mount.

Put shaving cream on your face
Then shave your face real close.
If your hair is balding on top
Don a hat—and then pose.

Wrinkles are shadowed with a hat.
Your face will softly glow.
Follow these orders to the "T"
Then listen to and fro.

People will see the hat first thing
Then see your smiling face.
They'll say, "*Oh my, you look so young!*"
Take compliments with grace.

Have a wonderful birthday!
(PS: The advice is for when you get much older).

Birthday Angel

Wishing that the birthday angel
Shine on you today.
Bringing you much happiness . . . and
Joy along the way.

Have a great day!

How Old Are You Mr. President

If you didn't know how old you were,
How old would you be?
Would you hobble thru the Whitehouse
And say *Woe is me?*

I think you're more like Satchel Paige
An icon I'm told
Because he didn't know his age
Played baseball quite old.

Attitude says much about you
Happy and serene.
Sixty years—not a huge plateau
With God in the scene.

Even if you might not feel like Satchel Paige,
Have a great birthday!

CHILDREN/GRANDCHILDREN

My Son So Far Away

Dear son so sweet I miss you so
This day and every day.
I long to see those sparkling eyes
To watch you hard at play.

My little son I love you much.
Your absence saddens me.
I miss the patter of your feet,
Your words that gladden me.

I miss that little impish smile.
Those devilish looks? Oh yes!
And recognize the warmth you bring
In thoughts of tenderness.

I visualize my little son
Another you love dear
But be a good boy, think of me
And wipe away that tear.

Chuck Perry and Snoopy 1971

The Paper Boy

My memory of you as a boy
When you were only eleven
The papers you delivered each day
All total days of seven.

You did a great job. Yes you did
With Snoopy by your side.
It taught you responsibility—
With that came lots of pride.

The ethics you now use today—
They are beyond compare
And I am just so proud of you
You really have a flair.

So keep on doing what you do
As long as you still can
But don't forget the memory
Of when it all began.

Little One

My precious little one with angelic blue eyes
And dimples in your cheeks, but impish little sighs.
You fill me with laughter when you play peek-a-boo
But fill me with sadness when you cry, *Boo-hoo-hoo!*

When morning comes to call and no one is smiling
You always change all that with charm so beguiling.
What would our house be like, without you little one?
Full of much emptiness, because you are our *sun*.

Coach Willie

Some people touch your life—I ponder why?
But no matter the years that have gone by
You just don't forget the good things they did
Especially for my shy little kid.

He knocked on our door one Saturday morn
And coaxed my shy little boy—second born—
To go play baseball on his new formed team.
And off they went to the start of a dream.

So how many games did they win or lose?
That mem'ry is gone, but what I'd still choose
Is a special coach to give out some joy
To the mother—and that shy little boy.

A Heartfelt Lesson

I walked into my sixteen-year old son, Curt's English classroom—where I was to start the evening's open house proceedings—and introduced myself to his teacher, Mrs. Knight. She was very pleasant-looking, fortyish and about 5'2". She directed me to Curt's desk where I sat down and tried to get as comfortable as I could for an overweight woman in a desk obviously made for young slim people.

Mrs. Knight warmly welcomed us parents and gave a short talk on what was expected of our children in sophomore English. She said that the students had left some of their schoolwork for us to look at. I thumbed through the papers and noticed the good grades Curt had received and that made me very proud.

As I started reading one of the papers, I couldn't believe my eyes. There was the missing puzzle piece—from an event that happened at Washington Junior High School, in Pekin in 1981, when Curt was twelve. It was his first day at the new school. We had just moved July Fourth weekend from East Peoria, where he went to Robein Grade School, from kindergarten to fourth grade. He was an extremely shy honor student, who loved school and had many friends at Robein.

Curt was out of his comfort zone when we moved to Pekin. Something happened that first day of school, and I had to drag him to school every day thereafter, while he was crying and saying he didn't want to go. He wouldn't tell me why. I had wished so bad that I could make his hurting go away, or suffer the hurt for him, but that's not what life is all about. As part of life each of us must bear our own pain of heartfelt lessons in some form or another.

On that English paper, was the answer I had wondered about for four years. Tears welled up in my eyes, as I read how some big boys on the bus—that first day of school—sprawled across the seats and wouldn't let him sit down. Curt had to stand all the way to school. He must have felt like everyone was staring at him. Kids can be so cruel sometimes. The children only added to his apprehension of a new town and going to a new school. That first day in 1981 was the last time he rode a school bus. He fussed so much I promised him if he would go to school, I would drive him there every day, so he wouldn't have to ride the bus anymore. I had a very stressful job at the time and put in 60 to 80 hours a week usually, but the extra time I spent driving him to school was worth it to ease Curt's pain a bit. When his friend Leonard got his driver's license he picked Curt up every day after that.

It was so heartbreaking watching Curt go through that torment. I never gave it a thought that Curt would have a problem adjusting to the new school or town. It was a lesson I will never forget.

Reminiscing

Your birthday is a special time
For me to reminisce
About the day when you were born
When I was filled with bliss.

But oh the first time I saw you—
"This could not be my son.
There must have been a big mistake."
The nurse said, "No, there's none."

You were so cute and chubby then.
That's why I was surprised.
You couldn't be my newborn babe,
But oh what big blue eyes!

What I remember most of you
When you were just a tike,
Was your happy disposition.
That's really what I liked.

I miss those baseball games so much.
The good times that we had
On trips to see the Cardinals play
Or jaunts to see Six Flags.

Until the Sandman Comes

God sent a special angel down who warms
And tickles my insides thru day and night
And when I tuck him in to sleep his charms
Encompass me and fill me with delight.

And when his dreams are full of sugarplums
Or turtles, puppies, even kitty cats,
It truly gets me thru the daily glums
Of when I scarce to hear his pitter pats.

If I could freeze these moments for awhile
I'd savor ev'ry little bitty kiss
For it would be so grand I would beguile
Away the time and have contented bliss.

So till the sandman touches his wee eyes
Dear Lord, I'll sing him heartfelt lullabies.

Believing

When I was growing up
I thought I had it pretty rough.
I was worried about little things
Like would it rain when I wanted to go swimming?
Or what would I wear to the coming dance?
Or who would feed Alphie, my rabbit?
Things weren't as complicated as they seemed to me back then.

When I grew up and had children of my own
Only then could I fully understand
Or appreciate my upbringing.
I received many wonderful life lessons
From some real experts—my siblings.
Now that I've experienced them, I want you—my children
To learn those same life lessons.
I want you to grow up with all of the tools
Needed to succeed.
I want you to understand what it means to work hard
For what's important in your life.

I want you to know that you must never give up
On the things you're passionate about
No matter how difficult it seems to be;
For it is in believing in your dreams
That they really can come true.

Oil on canvas Cheyenne & Ethan Perry 2002

Blessings

For little ones so full of love
I've waited oh, so long.
The joy they've brought into my world
Just fills my heart with song.

To feel them cuddle in my arms
And squeeze me oh so tight,
I sing with joy some fav'rite tunes
When I tuck them in at night!

Some days when I am full of stress.
I don't know up from down,
But when I gaze my eyes on them,
I just can't keep a frown.

And when I'm feeling kind of low
I search deep down inside
To where I tucked my grandkids in.
I'm *grandly* satisfied!

Cheyenne

When I first laid my eyes on you
How precious and so sweet.
The prettiest babe I'd ever seen
Oh what a special treat.

You really touched my heart that day
As I held you in my arms
And 'cause you were my first grandchild
Oh, how I felt your charms.

And for a grandchild oh so dear
Whose love I treasure most;
Just like when your dad was born
Of this I sure can boast.

I miss you much—it saddens me—
Because you're far away
But know that you are in my heart
On any given day.

So when I miss you I just reach
Into my heart and feel
That you are with me anyway
And that is such a deal.

Spiderman the Sleuth

Unlikely guy—Peter Parker—was he
Who had his own secret identity.
People that knew him would be quite surprised
T'know he was Spiderman—big, strong and wise.

I saw Spiderman crawl down from the roof
Put on his spider mask, become quite aloof.
What would they say if they knew the real truth?
"That Spiderman is certainly some sleuth."

The Race

Doc Hudson, Tow Mater and Flo were there
As well as lots of parts and tires for spare.
Little cars, big cars, blue ones and red
Some so souped up they smoked as they sped.

Sally watched the race from her fav'rite spot.
Number 95 is really hot.
That's Lightning McQueen (the fastest of all).
He reached the finish like a cannonball.

Nicholas Charles

An awesome treasure to behold,
Is little Nicholas Charles.
He'll bring us more than wealth untold,
His worth? There'll be no quarrels.

He may not be an astronaut,
Nor run for state election.
But he'll be tops no matter what,
He'll ne'er want for affection.

So take this little guy on home,
Love him oh so tenderly.
Wherever he decides to roam,
I will feel so *splendorly.*

A Birthday Tale

I was watching the kids one day when I was visiting my son, Chuck and his wife Denise in Highlands Ranch, Colorado. Denise had given Ethan a little baggy with a mixture of nuts and M & M's in it. Ethan came up to me later with a sad look on his face and said, "Grandma, the M & M's are all gone." He'd eaten all of the candy and left the nuts untouched. He thought maybe Grandma wouldn't know why the M & M's were gone and maybe give him more candy.

Grandsons are special; but I can't deny.
When they get in trouble they wonder why?
Like anything wrong they just couldn't do—
Sweet innocent looks that they give to you.

Grandsons might have dreams of Nascar racing,
Football, baseball, Ju Jitsu embracing.
No matter what they do you can be sure
There's no disappointment that Grandma can't cure.

Who is Brett Favre Anyway?

Penalties, touchdowns are part of the game.
Cleats and jerseys will not be the same
When Ethan goes out on the field tonight
He'll run and run with all of his might.

Brett Favre he is not, but you can be sure
When Ethan is out there he won't be demure.
Watch out for Ethan whatever you do—
Where did that ball go? He won't have a clue.

Natasha

I have a special wish for you
That all your dreams come true;
For you bring so much joy to me
I'm lucky to have you.

It seems like only yesterday
I held you in my arms.
When you were such a tiny girl
Oh—how I felt your charms.

Ariel's Plight

There was a young mermaid
Down deep in the sea.
She had gorgeous long hair
As red as can be.

She and her friend flounder
Roamed the ocean wide.
Then she met a human—
Yearned to be his bride.

She soon became a human.
Left her friends below.
So she could wed the prince.
She was all aglow.

Sydney's Monkey

There once was a monkey
As cute as he can be.
He also was funny
And lived in a tree.

Had a friend named Sydney
And he loved her so.
He made to her a plea—
"Your friend's got to go."

No monkeying around Sydney,
Have a great birthday!

. . . And Kitty Cat Too

Kitty Cat I love you much. You're sweet in ev'ry way.
So cuddly and comforting when I'm inside all day.
You're there when I'm feeling sad and also when I'm sick.
When I sometimes snap at you, you never say a lick.

You've a heart I can't resist and eyes that look so sweet,
But come to me so dismal when I sit down to eat.
Kitty cat, my favorite friend, when I pray 'for I sleep,
I always add, *and Kitty Cat too* and thank the Lord a heap.

Mira—A Baby Dear

Our babies are a precious gift.
They're filled with so much love.
There's nothing like them in this world
That comes from up above.

Enfold her in your arms real tight.
Smother her with kisses.
And treasure this sweet little one.
She'll fill all your wishes.

FRIENDSHIP

"Each friend represents a world in us, a world possibly not born until they arrive, and it is only by this meeting that a new world is born." Anis Nin (1903–1977), French/American writer

A Friend Is . . .

One you can pour out your heart to
And she always understands.
One who can make you happy
Just being with you.
One who can keep a secret
If you ask her to.
One who has such a giving spirit
When she might not have much herself.
One you can always count on
To lend a helping hand.
One who shows such compassion
For those less fortunate.
One who you know loves you
Even though she might not tell you so.
One who has left a lasting impression
In other people's hearts.
One who will be missed
When she goes to be with God.
One who will never be forgotten
Because she's always been my friend.

Just For Today

I treasure your friendship.
It means more to me than words could ever say.
God might choose to take you from me tomorrow
But I have you right now—this very minute—
Today!

You are a gift from God to be enjoyed to the ultimate.
Even if I lose you tomorrow
I'll savor every moment I have you for my friend;
For your friendship has enriched my life.

Tomorrow someone else might need
Your friendship more than I
Or maybe we can share you together.
No matter what tomorrow brings,
You are mine—right now—
Today!

I thank God each and every day I have you for a friend
And maybe God will lend you to me for more than
Just a day or two,
Because I really need you!
I need your fellowship!
I need your acceptance of me, no matter what.

As my friend, you understand me better than I do myself.
You give me room to breathe and room for mistakes.
You realize I'm not perfect,
But understand that I'm always striving for perfection.
You laugh when I laugh.
You cry when I cry.
You lift me up when I am down.
When I have negative thoughts
You help me turn them into something positive.
You help me realize that through the positive power

Of Jesus Christ all things are possible.
You accept me for who I am
Not for whom you wish me to be.
You allow me to be myself.
You listen to me!
You let me tell you how I feel even if you don't agree with me—
Heaven knows you can't possibly agree with me all the time.
You love me *just because!*

You are truly my friend for a day—
Right now—this very minute.
But of all the things you are to me
I want to be to you also.
Because it takes both of us doing these things together
To make up a friendship so special as ours.
It's special because God is the center of it.

May God bless you, my friend.
When you leave me may God replace you with another
Just like you;
For you are as important to my well being
As food is to my body
And God is to my soul.
God is forever!
You are for today!
And I thank God for you, my friend
Just for today!

Betty

Betty loved the song, "His Eye Is on the Sparrow"
I think of her every time I hear that beautiful song.
It puts a song in my own heart too.

Betty was my friend since high school
Then I worked with her at Caterpillar.
She was such a special friend and very smart.

Many years later she touched the hearts of many
With her strength and courage
As she battled bone cancer.

I felt honored and blest to be included
In her vast circle of friends.
She loved hearts and teddy bears
And every time I see a heart
Or teddy bear
I think of Betty.

. . . And Teddy Bear Too

Teddy Bear I love you much. You're sweet in ev'ry way.
So cuddly and comforting when I'm inside all day.
You're there when I'm feeling low and also when I'm sick.
When things seem to fall apart, you never say a lick.

Sitting on my shelf at night, you never say a word,
Along with all my other friends—even Tweety Bird.
Little bear, my fav'rite friend, when I pray 'for I sleep,
I always add, *and Teddy Bear too,* and thank the Lord a heap.

The Rose Garden—New Life Christian Singles

One evening a few years ago, I walked into a rose garden. It wasn't so much the beauty that was seen there, but more the beauty that was felt from within; for this wasn't a typical garden. It was God's garden and the roses were actually people—Christian people.

I didn't find it easy to walk into the garden that night. Those roses were disguised as people and people scared me half to death. The fear was short-lived, because once inside that garden, the petals started unfolding and out blossomed the most beautiful people I had ever met.

The warmth and love I experienced is hard to explain. It wasn't something I could actually see or touch. It was just there in the air. The presence of the Holy Spirit was very evident to me that night.

Now I know what Christianity is all about. It's about warmth, love, empathy, compassion and all those things God wants us to have for one another. It's about people willing to share the good times, the bad times, the laughing, the crying, the joys and the hurts. It's for teaching us to cope; how to face the realities of everyday living; how to turn our stumbling blocks into stepping-stones. It's for teaching us that through the positive power of Jesus Christ all things are possible.

I feel fortunate to be one of God's chosen ones and thank Him every day for the opportunity to experience just a little bit of heaven here on earth.

Lilies

Consider the Lilies

The Lord is calling.
He has something important
For you and me to do.
Walk with me into the fields.

We are going
Where many others have not trod
Go with me into the fields.

You must be thinking
I am not qualified.
But the Lord will send the Holy Spirit,
The Comforter, to walk with us
To inspire us, to guide us.
Toil with me in the fields.

"Look at the lilies
They don't toil and spin,
And Solomon in all his glory
Was not robed as well as they are...
Your heavenly Father knows your needs.
He will always give you all you need
From day to day
If you will make the Kingdom of God
Your primary concern."

The crops are plentiful
The laborers are few
Come with me into the fields.

Afterword

A friend gave me a plaque when I was going through a tough time and I applied that saying to my own life. I learned the importance of never giving up. I keep the plaque where I will see it every day as a reminder to me. It says:

"You may not always reach your goal, but there's recompense in trying.

Horizons broaden so much more the higher you are flying."

Author unknown

Conclusion

If we do the best job possible in all things, no matter where we end up—and no matter what someone else might think of us—we will be a success in the eyes of God. There can be only one winner in a race, but if we don't try at all, we'll never know what we could have achieved. We just need to be diligent in every aspect of our lives. Babe Ruth—one of the greatest ball players of all time—was a wonderful example of that. People always remember the 714 homeruns he hit, but Ruth had 1330 strikeouts—almost twice as many of the amount of homeruns. It's just a matter of not giving up no matter what the odds seem to be and that can be applied to almost anything we do.

Bibliography of References

Albom, Mitch, author of *For One More Day*

Downing, Eileen, mother of General Wayne Downing

Fortune, Marlianne Downing, sister of the general

McEnany, Brian, Wayne's classmate at USMA Class of 1962

Osbeck, Kenneth W., author of *101 Hymn Stories*

Peoria Journal Star, March 23, 1958

Peoria Star, February 14, 1934

Swindoll, Charles R. *Growing Strong in the Seasons of Life*

Ten Boom, Corrie, author of *The Hiding Place* along with John & Elizabeth Sherrill

Yap, Mike, Wayne's classmate at USMA Class of 1962

CPSIA information can be obtained at www.ICGtesting.com
Printed in the USA
LVOW112301100412

277031LV00001B/74/P